Laura Payne is a mindfulness practitioner and teacher. A former journalist, broadcaster and businesswoman working across all aspects of the media, including newspapers, magazines, radio and TV, she is now a clinical psychotherapist & supervisor, living and working in private practice in London, UK.
She runs Mindfulness Leadership
(www.mindfulnessleadership.co.uk), a business aimed at introducing mindful techniques to the workplace.

Under The Lime Tree

NINE STEPS TO A MINDFUL LIFE
(Without Meditating)

LAURA PAYNE

Onefulness Publishing

Onefulness

First published in Great Britain in 2016 by Onefulness

Published by Onefulness Publishing ©
London, England

www.onefulness.com

ISBN: 978-0-9954889-0-8 (paperback)

To Mark, Nats and Rae
And all my guides. You know who you are!
Thank you for the inspiration under the Lime Tree.

CONTENTS

Acknowledgments

Where do you start with thank-you's especially when a book has been a lifetime in germinating? My family and friends have always been my greatest inspiration, as well as my spiritual practices over the years. So I'm truly grateful for all of your thoughts, impact and generosity during my life. We have been under this Lime Tree for a long time.

I first discovered meditation during a yoga class a thousand years ago with Iyengar yogini, Marigold Norman, an amazing teacher whose work was continued by the wonderful Jean Cosham. They were both inspiring. Along the way I would also like to thank my spiritual circle friends, especially Karen Shreeve, Evelyn McDonald, Julie Bushell, Diana Williams, Wendy Cadman & Jan Reid.

In recent years I would like to thank all those I've met in the modern day mindfulness movement but especially Emeritus Professor Mark Williams of the Oxford Mindfulness Centre and all his dedicated team. Your eight week MBCT programme was a great step on the way. I would also like to thank Jon Treanor who joined me in Mindfulness Leadership, a venture to take mindfulness out into the workplace.

My introduction to equine therapy was down to psychotherapist Sally Hudson. It was a magical and game-changing experience.

Thank you to Onefulness and those who advised on the publication, including Mark Perrow, Natalie Miles, Rachel Miles and Beverly Hurwitz. A particular huge thanks to Marie and David Skilling for all their design and production input.

Thanks also to some special spiritual influences on the recent path: Mark Perrow, Kim 'Shams' Richardson, Aziz Dikeulias, Nigel Hamilton and to Aziza Scott, who led that insightful retreat under the Lime Tree in La Hublais, France.

INTRODUCTION
Down the passage which we did not take
Towards the door we never opened
Into the rose-garden.

Burnt Norton, T.S. Eliot.

I sat under the lime tree as the morning sun danced on the leaves and noticed the tension in my chest, my awkward breathing and my mind flitting from problem to problem. I was unable to settle into the peace and tranquillity of what was a beautiful rose garden in a retreat centre in Brittany, France.

I'd come there to spend five days in silence - a treat I had discovered several years ago that brought re-centring and balance back in my life.

Some friends and colleagues laughed when they heard about my first retreat. 'You? Spend five days in silence?' I realised they didn't really know me.

Despite years of corporate presentations and dealing with people I'd found that I was very comfortable in my own space, either shared in the powerful collective holding of a group retreat, or in the deeper well of one's mind, body and soul on an individual retreat. I embraced the solitude of being shut away in a room with someone bringing you food and meditation practices once a day.

Since then retreats have become an essential feature of my life, once or twice a year. Yet here I was, in France, unable to find that essential calm and peace.

I sat with my agitation. It mounted in my chest. My heart started to pound. I couldn't get comfortable. I looked enviously at fellow retreatants who'd adopted stations of annoying Zen-like calm in various parts of the garden. What was wrong with me? I was normally like them: tuned into the stillness of my meditation practice; at one with life in all its glory round me.

INTRODUCTION

Giving my mind permission to hit the negative button meant powerful doubts, fears, self-critical thoughts and judgements poured into my being. Very soon I was well down that heavily-trod garden path of feeling a failure, not being good-enough, not fitting in, panicking about all I should be doing, hadn't done, could have done. The list soon became endless...

And then I stopped. I noticed my language had slipped into the conditional tense of 'would have, could have, should have'. Over the years I have learned these are the warning cues that I'm not being present which, of course, unsurprisingly, requires the present tense: the language of the here and now.

I'd slipped out of the calm garden of mindfulness and into the chaotic world of the busy, over-worked everyday life that I'd come to leave behind. Yet I hadn't escaped. Somehow these uncomfortable bedfellows had hitched a lift and were enjoying a sneaky trip away.

Indignant, I wanted to know how I'd got into this state. For goodness sake, I was a mindfulness teacher. I had years of practices under my spiritual belt since I was first introduced to meditating through yoga when my children were young. In that period, twenty years ago, I was running one the UK's top seventy communication consultancies, serving global FTSE 100 clients, alongside juggling the demands of a young family.

During that time I finally recognised that something had to change dramatically when I once pulled up in the car outside my daughter's school, power-dressed in my office finery and I turned round to my daughter in the back and wondered incredulously why she wasn't wearing her school uniform. At that moment she piped up: 'Mummy, why are we at school? It's Saturday and I thought we were going to shops.'

I looked at her, puzzled, and then at my clothes. And then it dawned. It was a Saturday. She was right. We were meant going to the supermarket. I had simply slipped into the autopilot that had become my life. It was, for me, a massive wake-up call, that so many report on their Damascus conversion road to mindfulness. I went on to find yoga and, in the process, a whole new mindset.

Now, sitting under this magnificent tree, recalling my recent life leading up to this retreat, I realised that I'd allowed many of my established practices to slip during a newly-found increased busy period. Life had become fraught. The concept of quality me-time had subtly morphed into a rolling of one meeting to another, a series of snatched phone calls with family and friends, and several serious diary clashes, with me missing important appointments or making them by the skin of my teeth.

In effect, despite the odd bit of meditation here or there, I'd ironically stopped being properly mindful.

I'd become locked in a spiral of frantic doing. The more I did, the less impact I seemed to make. And then the more seemed to need doing. I was worried I wasn't keeping up with the demands of emails, website management, social media, speaking to, or seeing friends, my family, which meant I would beat myself up even further about my lack of apparent coping skills. This then fuelled the downward spiral even further. I was trapped in the classic exhaustion funnel which we discuss in mindfulness classes.

Even in this beautiful garden I was still worried about what I should be doing; should I do my practice, should I go for a mindful walk, should I go back to my bedroom for a sleep, should I relax and lay-out in the sun, should I, should I...??

I'd brought the incessant nagging voice of the relentless Doer with me. I'd converted it from Doing in my everyday life to Doing on the retreat. I had stopped Being. In fact, I had almost stopped Being all together...

Before I'd left for France I'd got myself into such a state I'd made myself ill and my partner, worried I might be having a heart attack, had called the paramedics. As I looked back, lounging in the retreat sun, I realised the illness was simply the result of tension I'd been manifesting over several months.

This enormous realisation brought me up sharp. It brought me back to the building blocks of my mindfulness practice. It made me revisit it with eyes anew and, more importantly, made me critically consider what actually constitutes a mindful life.

Ancient and modern Buddhist priests believe that life's challenge is how we can spend each moment in a state of continuous awareness, in effect a living meditation. This is about making the whole of one's life a meditation, not just those precious, preserved moments crossed-legged on the floor. For the priest this is a fundamental aspect of living a life of devotion.

INTRODUCTION

Many of today's mindfulness movement's concepts have actually evolved from some of these ancient practices of contemplation and observation to slow life down.

So, I was left pondering: if mindfulness is not just about sitting meditating what are its essential qualities that ensure we truly live our lives – rather than simply rushing through them?

How do we bring mindfulness into the very fibre of our existence from the moment we wake until we return to bed at night? And by doing so what are the benefits?

The following nine steps in this book are the fruit of that wonderful simple moment, pondering under the lime tree. They are a guide as to how we can live a mindful life without meditating (in the traditional sense of sitting in stillness). As you will find, it is an interesting challenge.

So how to approach this book? Each step is broken down in its own chapter, complete with some easy exercises to help you practise and develop the 'mindful muscle' required to explore fully the recommended mindful practices. You might find it easier to read the whole chapter and then go back to try out the exercises or do some of them as you go along.

You might choose to hop around the various chapters. Perhaps you prefer a non-linear approach to life. Or perhaps you prefer the comfort of structure and enjoy working through the book step by step. It doesn't matter. Mindfulness is very much about curiosity and self-observation, without judgement or criticism, questioning and challenging the mindsets you bring through habit or convention or upbringing, to various aspects of your life.

Whatever your approach all the steps build and interlock into a contemplation of what constitutes a mindful life for you. If you want to learn more about the world's key mindfulness communities and approaches there is a breakdown at the end of the book, as well as a summary of the exercises. And, perhaps after trying out some of the practices you will find that you are ready to sit down and simply meditate so a sneaky Step Ten gives some tips on how to do just that.

In the end, enjoy exploring a mindful 'you' under the sun of your own lime tree of life...

STEP ONE
Treat Each Day As If It's Your Last
What might have been and what has been
Point to one end, which is always present.

Burnt Norton, T. S. Eliot.

So what if I had died that day at home before I left for the retreat? And if I should die in the next few minutes what recollections of my life would be in those last flashing moments? If I believed in reincarnation what would I want to take with me and remember from today?

Locked in the Doing Mode, especially in the West, with so much emphasis on achieving, having a successful life, and simply 'having', in a bid to keep the consumer economies ticking over with our getting and spending, we forget to 'be'.

We lurch from moment to moment in what the mindfulness community fondly calls autopilot. In reality that means we live a life whereby there is no present – it's a mixture of what's next, 'the future', or what's happened, 'the past', not what's 'now'.

We power on doing what we do. We spend so much time in our head we're simply not engaged with life. For instance, as with my school example, we drive somewhere and wonder how we got there, or we don't get on with the planned task at work but get side-tracked by emails or play on our mobile phone or tablet.

Mindfulness gives us the tools and the permission to stop and listen to the mind's chatter that hijacks our very existence.

I will discuss this further in Step Three which looks deeper into the state of autopilot but for now just take a step back and reflect on some of the 'voices' that persistently crowd your day and jostle for attention. Many of these voices have taken root over the years since childhood and become like mini sub-personalities, conditioning and controlling our thinking and behaviour.

STEP ONE

See if you can name these: planner, problem solver, organiser, pacifier, boss, fantasiser, daydreamer, critic, judge both of self and others.

I often joke when I run mindfulness sessions that this is not mindfulness; this is not about the mind. It's bodyfulness, it's about re-incorporating the whole of you, mind, body and soul, with hopefully brief brushes of onefulness, the term I jokingly use for those sweet moments when it suddenly all comes together; moments which equate with a deeper sense of joy and meaning.

Often, it takes a crisis in our lives, usually involving a life or death moment, to pull us up sharp as we are confronted by a brutal reawakening to a real sense of the now.

I remember vividly the horrific night of my father's sudden death. He was just fifty-nine and died of a violent heart attack on the sitting room floor. My frightened mother had struggled in vain to revive him as paramedics coaxed her, via the phone, to attempt CPR.

From the minute I took the call about his death I can recall each moment by moment with the utmost clarity, even now twenty years on. From the overwhelming smell of putting fuel in my car to make the long drive to my parents' home, to the paradoxical joy of seeing my dad's favourite camellias in bloom outside their front door.

Weirdly, at that moment I was fully alive, so much so it is deeply imprinted on the whole of myself, not just in my head as a thought-memory but in the core of my very existence. Even now, as I recall the smell of the petrol, I can sense the gag reflex rising in my throat.

Twentieth century American psychologist, Alfred Maslow, called these instances 'peak moments', when someone is deeply in harmony with himself and his surroundings. He saw them as part of self-actualisation, which encapsulates the concept of reaching our full potential through a quest for knowledge, creativity and spiritual enlightenment. For the majority of people these moments would be rare but Maslow believed that a self-actualised person would have them daily Berger, 1983, p.43).[1]

Peak moments for me are moments of deeper connection; a transcendence of our notions of time and space into something more universal, more spiritual, which profoundly feeds the soul.

STEP ONE

When teaching mindfulness I sometimes do an exercise called 'When Time Stood Still' and ask people to recall a moment in their lives that resonates with this.

Try it now for yourself:

Close your eyes, settle into your chair, place your feet flat on the floor and just listen and connect to your breathing for three breaths. Then say to yourself: 'When time stood still I...' Where were you? Who were you with? What did you think and feel, and what sensations were in your body or are now rising as you do the exercise? Sit with whatever arises and then analyse what happens to you under these categories: Body Sensations, Emotions, Thoughts and Actions.

Peak moments often recalled by participants include the birth of a child, a deep connection with nature, or with art (visual arts, music or literature), falling in love, sexual ecstasy, personal achievements whether at work, in sport, or in life in general, religious or profound spiritual moments. Not all the experiences are happy, several are traumatic, like the moments after my father's death.

The key is that they are powerfully imprinted on our sense of self and bring us back into a genuine connection with who and what we are. Very often they significantly change our lives.

These moments can contain one another, like Russian dolls. When I lay on the bathroom floor just before my retreat, struggling to breathe with a crushing pain in my chest, I reconnected with my dad's death. More importantly, I remembered a greater overwhelming moment in my late teens when I'd had a near death experience (NDE). To believe you are dying certainly fulfils the 'when time stood still' criteria and becomes distinctly life-changing.

No-one really knew what had happened. It was a Sunday evening and relatives from Wales had come to our London home for the weekend. I don't remembered feeling particularly agitated or stressed but suddenly I found my heart was racing and I was struggling to breathe.

As I sat in an armchair in our sitting room I knew I was dying. I gently slipped from a very physical and painful state of fear and panic spreading throughout my whole body into a wonderful, peaceful acceptance that I was going to die. And I was happy.

This calm had a deep sense of inevitability as I left my body and found that I could look down on a very worried and panicking family below. I can still remember their faces clearly and feeling very sad for them, sad they could not understand that I was safe and, in fact, feeling incredibly peaceful and free from the tension of life with its struggles and choices.

Like many who've experienced an NDE this sadness of the inability to communicate this sense of well-being to those left behind is well reported.

How can you explain the surreal nature of an NDE? Neuroscientific and physiological attempts to fathom this experience still have no concrete findings. However, most NDE accounts share similar details to those I will outline.

As you fade from this plane an immense joyful ecstasy spreads into the fibre of your Self which now seems to have no physical form. You are pure consciousness. For me, it suddenly seemed like a flood of light had irradiated my being and all around me. Many have likened this to a tunnel of light but that doesn't do justice to what can only be called the light of lights. Its purity was dazzling. Its power that of the deepest healing.

I felt an all-pervading sense of love surge through my being, a love that bound me so that I wanted to remain in its power for eternity and yet offered the deepest sense of freedom.

Within this light-being, because in some way it felt like a pulsating life-form, were what seemed like hundreds of other beings, the closest including faces of those in the family that I knew had died. My grandmother, who had recently passed, stood at the opening of the light and we spoke.

She told me I didn't have to stay. It wasn't my time and I could choose to return to the physical life plane. But she was insistent that it was my 'choice'. I was reluctant to go. This was beauty beyond all my experience. This was home. She reminded me of the plans I'd made for the life which, until then, had stretched out before me and I could feel their 'tug' again.

I chose to return.

At that moment it was suddenly all over and I found myself back in my body, deafened by the loud commotion of anxiety around me and a deepened connection with breathing cool air into my very self at a cellular level. I never knew if I'd been gone seconds, minutes or hours. Time had definitely stopped still...

Ambulances and doctors had been called. Various pontifications ranged from a possible heart-attack, some odd pulmonary crisis or a huge panic attack. 'Who knows? Who cares?' I thought, lying dazed on the sofa, watching bemused as my family screamed, crashed and banged around me in panic; lying there calmly, in my own oasis of a deeper sense of 'knowing'. My parents sensibly opted for a 'wait and see' approach rather than a dash to hospital as I was obviously suddenly much better.

For me, I had returned to life and all I wanted to do was to get on with it. Over the years I recognised that the decision to 'return' encompassed the most fundamental existential choice: whether to live or die. The will to live once made and chosen at a profound level is intoxicating and empowering.

From then, I threw myself whole-heartedly into living life to the full, making big choices and making big mistakes along the way. I realised life wasn't about getting it right but simply getting on with it. As a teenager I decided to *treat each day as my last*.

Now, back in the retreat garden, lying under the lime tree, I tuned back into my teenage self and revisited that moment with the Angels, as I often privately called it.

Strangely, I'd found over the years most people would back off when, depending on appropriate conversations, I tentatively mentioned that I'd had a Near Death Experience. Their lack of curiosity surprised me at first. I would ponder on people's lack of interest until I realised that, instead of it being about disbelief, their fear was really about talking or hearing about death.

Death is simply not something discussed in the West. And yet, as the much-quoted adage goes the only certainties in life paradoxically are death...and taxes.

I find in my psychotherapy practice that we all spend our lives constructing elaborate structures and mechanisms to one concrete end – beating death. From the moment we are born we are involved in the existential struggle of survival: how to stay alive and what that means.

These early learned structures, as defences and resistances, serve us well against the onslaughts of childhood but this struggle becomes sophisticated and complex as the constructs mature and take root. Like the fabled screaming mandrake root they can be nearly impossible to pull out. These defences usually become the 'voices' we discussed earlier which crowd our minds and deafen our life.

All fears, phobias, anxieties and depressions can be traced back in some way to death, lurking like a ghost in the human machine. From the minute we get a sense of our own mortality, at whatever age, we are constructing our defences paradoxically against the inevitable, against the yawning gap of the unknown, the bottomless pit of non-existence. It can be simply terrifying to accept the finality of death.

The leading existential American psychiatrist Irving Yalom, looks at how the concepts surrounding our existential concerns, are manifested in our personality and in our relationship with life. From childhood, he states, we seek reassurance about death from our care-givers which is often lacking and so have to learn to deal with death until we develop 'efficient and sophisticated forms of denial' (Yalom, 1980. P.91)[2].

Some of the favourite death denial packages I have encountered include: having children and creating or continuing a lineage, an extension of this is leaving an inheritance or legacy of some kind behind, being recognised as 'special' (positive and negative) which can include being famous, infamous or being renowned in one's field, writing a book, music, creating art work, or in some way making a mark on history.

Can you identify what's yours?

Whatever our plan we spend the rest of our life pursuing our chosen struggle against death.

Sometimes when I work with clients who flirt with death through addiction or reckless behaviour we reach a deep, existential moment in the therapeutic space when the client's reasons for choosing life have stagnated and meaning has become lost due to a whole complex web of reasons which underpin addiction.

I then challenge the client by asking: "What is your relationship with death?" I've often wondered if it should be the other way round: "What's your relationship with life?" but have realised that this is the tenuous issue. Death is a simpler and less demanding friend.

And so, in the end, as I lay in the retreat rose garden under the lime tree I came to the conclusion that the only defence against death is to live a life full of meaning, and the only way to live a life of meaning is to live being true to your values.

Note, this is about values, not goals. As part of the Western 'doing' world we are adamantly focused on our goals. Happiness is measured by what we perceive as our achievements. These are invariably external and material: the latest gadget, next car, bigger house, better job. Businesses and organisations are obsessed with goal attainment, usually financial, as the definition of success. We all have targets and goals to hit.

The key aspect here is the external nature of this kind of goal-orientated definition of happiness. We often hear the phrase the 'pursuit of happiness', implying we are chasing some elusive quality which, when pinned down, will magically give our lives deeper meaning. But apart from the inevitable annual workplace appraisal question: 'Are you happy in your job?' how do you define what makes you happy in the workplace or at home?

While we are chasing our autopilot tails, during a stressful round of phone calls, emails and meetings, does happiness lurk in that amazing deal you've landed, or is it found on your children's faces when you finally get home for the first time that week in time to tuck them into bed? Is it when we are out shopping for yet another pair of shoes, the latest gadget or beauty treatment? Or is it in giving to your favourite charity or joining a mentoring project for deprived school-kids?

Genetic scientists are now confirming what the ancient Greeks and eastern-based religions have understood for thousands of years that a fleeting state happiness does not confer the same depth of well-being that a more centred, internalised state can provide.

In fact, researchers at University of North Carolina and University of California (UCLA) (Wheeler, 2013)[3] have found that although Hedonism, the externalised pleasure principle part of life, is said to improve our happiness quotient, its deeper counterpart, Eudaimonia, the ancient Greek concept of a more contented internalised form of happiness, can actually change our bodies at a genetic level.

Looking at the biological influence of hedonic and eudemonic well-being through the human genome these scientists are interested in the pattern of gene expression within people's immune cells. They were surprised to find that eudemonic well-being was, indeed, associated with a significant decrease in the body's cell regulator gene, CTRA, which is affected by stress. In contrast, hedonic well-being was associated with a significant increase in the CTRA profile.

In other words, the hedonistic pursuit of happiness approach, a belief that happiness is something we *take* in from the outside world, is actually not good for our health and, long term, equates with stress. Whereas eudemonic projects, such as charitable giving or mentoring, make you feel good all over and leave a lasting and rewarding satisfaction because you *give* from within.

Before you start thinking: 'It's all Greek to me' consider what really creates meaning in the home or workplace?

How long are we really satisfied with corporate incentivising objects, packages and experiences, like the latest gadget, top of the range car or yet another expensive holiday before we crave, like all well-trained consumers, the next hedonistic 'fix'?

After the tough years of recession in western corporate life, executives and their families who've been financially ruined can answer that question easily.

Once the economic tsunami had washed away the external trappings of a wealth many executives found that they had to turn to something within, to the seed core of Being to discover something that is permanent and lasting; namely a meaningful, constant state to which one can always return safely whatever is happening in the exterior world; a state based on values not goals.

For me, this centring and rediscovery of our values lies at the heart of modern day mindfulness practices. This is about putting the right kind of happiness back on our daily agenda.

Lying on a mat in the warmth of the retreat garden I mindfully tuned into my whole sense of being. I lay fully in the moment exploring my bodily sensations, emotions, thoughts and desires to act. What would I have missed or taken with me from that retreat garden in La Hublais, France if it I were to treat this day as my last?

Immediately, the intense sweetness of the tiniest white roses from a nearby large bush filled the air around me. Breathing in this heady draught I felt my body sinking deeper in waves of growing calm into the mat.

I scrabbled to think of romantic poets I'd read who'd tried to capture this moment but, instead, found myself wanting to let go of intellectualising this softening experience. I watched the sunlight dance on the lime leaves canopy above me as the wind swirled the branches and then felt the mixture of warmth of the sun heat my skin and the opposing coolness of the breeze tease these heated patches. I thought I could lie here forever.

A fly joined me on my mat, buzzing and cleaning its black crunchy body. I remembered a battle with flies during a previous retreat in the Sinai desert and smiled at this connection with the past. However, I simply acknowledged the thought without allowing memories to hijack me from the present, breathing in to use my breath as an anchor to the here and now.

A pigeon in distant trees flapped its wings and flew over, a grey missile, determined on some course. Still I lay there, with no apparent course, no goal finally, except to be, sinking deeper into the ground supporting me. I perused the concept of this transfer of weight; that finally I had let go and was not supporting myself with all the psychological baggage that entailed, but had relaxed so much that the earth held me in its arms.

A sudden vulnerability of lying there in the open, feeling so exposed, was replaced with a sense of deeper nurturing and protection; a greater sense of trust. I could trust I was safe. I could trust that I had no need of plans or goals which transformed into worries and anxieties and a host of other emotions. I could be and still be cared for.

In that mindful moment I had connected with something beyond time and space. It was a connection with a collective consciousness, a oneness, or whatever you, personally, want to call that, which, for me, is represented by God. If this was my last day, I thought, this beauty would have made my life worthwhile. And the trauma of my life pre-retreat melted away into that ground.

I considered my values, not my goals, and found that the people I loved were paramount. If this was my last day what would I want to say to them?

I wrote a mental letter to everyone who was significant in my life. It became an interesting exploration of the meaning of love, forgiveness and repentance as I asked myself why I loved them, what made me happy that we were in each other's lives and why I would miss them.

By stripping away the daily niggles and issues that pervade all relationships this instance of authentic purity enabled me to reflect on the key qualities of my loved ones. And in that moment I truly saw them, as well as myself.

The scented rose air pervaded the whole of the retreat and constantly brought me back to this rediscovered stillness during the week. Its memory still brings me back today.

I went on to play with the concept of *'treating each day as if it's your last'*. In fact, becoming more playful and curious is an outcome of living a mindful life, and so I played.

After an afternoon of rain, I sheltered in a porch with other retreatants, watching it shower on life outside. I suddenly thought, if this were my last day so what if I got wet?

Like a child, barefoot, I bounced around the retreat garden instead of cowering, waiting for the rain to end. It was magical. My senses came alive as I connected with the squidgy feel of rain-laden moss between my toes, felt the dew of rain on my skin and heard its soothing drumming on the leaves. I wasn't simply observing the outside world. I was the outside world. Rain, grass, trees, garden, me. We were one. We were life. And it was intoxicating.

I look at this concept of mindful exploration in more depth in Step Seven: Stop Being Boring - Do Something Different Every Day.

This experience is not something you only access at magical moments, such as being on retreat, but can be part of living a daily mindful life. I've actively taken this concept *'treating each day as if it's your last'* into my life since. It helps monitor the censoring survival voice that helps protect us but also, when unfettered, this voice can stop the fun.

So how can you take this concept into your own life to ensure you are living it, not cruising it?

Right now check-in and ask yourself what are you doing in this moment? Wherever you are reading this breathe deeply three times and just sense the chair or bed or ground which is supporting you and connect with it. Then take the moment to reconnect with your body sensations, emotions, thoughts and desires to act. Tune in and ask yourself if this is my last day what would I take away with me from this moment? Savour the experience fully, watching what happens to you. There's no need to rush, let time look after itself. Allow life to meet you, absorb you, become you.

And then ask yourself, 'What do I value most?' Perhaps find three things you value; you might find more but don't strain to make a list or you will slip into the active 'doing' mode, just note what instantly comes to mind.

You can try writing a letter to loved ones. Ask why you love them, what makes you happy that you are in each other's lives and why you would miss them. See if you can sense the qualities that they hold and also any message that you would want to give them.

Perhaps plan to tune in three times each day to your experience, setting an alarm on your phone, to ask yourself, 'if this is my last day what would I take away from this experience?'

And if you are 'treating each day as if it's your last' what would you do differently today, what would need to change or be incorporated in some way?

Obviously these thoughts can spiral out into greater existential concerns about being in the right job, with the right person, in the right place. Allow the bigger thoughts to settle rather than unpick them right now. Just note they have surfaced and that you can return to them later.

In this moment it is about looking at the small ways we censor our actions, such as building routine responses or thoughts into our life. These structures are important and carry us through the day but can harness petty mindsets that stop us exploring or seeing our world anew.

Perhaps as an exercise go a new way home, eat something you wouldn't normally or wear something different. Note what comes to mind right now.

In the end life ticks on by and you want to make sure you are living it, not cruising it.

STEP TWO

STEP TWO
Go Slower

At the still point of the turning world. Neither flesh nor fleshless;
Neither from nor towards; at the still point, there the dance is,

Burnt Norton, T.S. Eliot.

We rush through life. One headlong plunge into the mass of doing. How often have you commented to friends and family about the speed of the passing year? 'Goodness! It's April already' or 'I can't believe I'm thinking about Christmas again?' I've heard so many people say to me, 'If only I had time,' or 'you're so lucky to find time to do that'.

Yet, when we stop to think about it, we all have time. And that's the clue: finding time to stop. In the daily hurtle which constitutes our lives we collapse into bed at night and wonder what happened to the day. Suddenly, we find we are wondering where the month and year have gone, and then our lives.

As a result, we often manically seize at life even more, cramming in more and more, in bid to make it more fulfilling, more meaningful, or just to get more done. More is the by-word here, it seems. When we feel we haven't met more of these tasks it is no surprise we encounter feelings of failure and uselessness.

We watch those around us who seem to time-manage effortlessly as they sail from task to task and from achievement to achievement. It's no wonder medics are recording record levels of stress and anxiety, and the darker condition: depression.

We're constantly taunted with media stories of the mother of seven who has a fabulous career as a CEO of industry and still fits in yoga, Pilates and cooks every night. Or the guy who works out at the gym every morning at 5am before going to the office to run several businesses and then, magically by night, becomes a guru or expert in art history – the ultimate renaissance man.

So driving on we go even faster. Foot down on life's accelerator and we're off, chasing the distant haze called multi-tasking.

16

Neurologists can now prove that the concept of multi-tasking is a myth. Apologies to all women who have long believed this one quality endows superiority over men. However, the brain just can't function properly if it's constantly switching between tasks, which is what happens when we think we are multi-tasking.

Earl K. Miller, a Picopower professor of neuroscience at MIT (Massachusetts Institute of Technology) runs one of the world's leading laboratories investigating the phenomenon of divided attention.[1]

Professor Miller uses experimental and theoretical approaches to study the neural basis of high-level cognitive functions that underlie complex goal-directed behavior. The focus is on the frontal lobe, the region of the brain most elaborated in humans.

The Miller laboratory has provided insights into how categories, concepts, and rules are learned, the nature of mental flexibility, how attention is focused, and how the brain co-ordinates thought and action. (earlkmiller.org, n.d.)

He has found that our brains are not wired to multitask well and can only take in the world in little bits and chunks at a time. Those who think themselves accomplished multitaskers are deluding themselves. They are actually just switching very rapidly from one task to another. As they cram in more and more the brain becomes exhausted from the over-processing of so much information.

The frontal lobe part of the brain is an "executive system" which enables this task-switching function. It exerts voluntary control over behavioral actions so while you are reading this you have probably checked your email, texts, perhaps googled something or could even be listening to music.

It's a bit like the conductor of an orchestra, demanding musicians to play in different styles: louder, softer, more staccato, faster, or slower. However, while something is being asked to play louder another aspect will have to dampen down or take a pause.

How often have you been on the phone to a friend, family member or even workplace caller and checked your emails? You think you are doing both tasks well but in fact the frontal lobe 'conductor' will be damping down one function at the expense of the other.

Perhaps your focus will be heightening the auditory aspect; so you concentrate on your friend's interesting story on the phone, only to find that you've sent a misspelt email. Or, you've tuned out of something important on the phone while trying to write an email.

Says Miller: "Those things are nearly impossible to do at the same time. You cannot focus on one while doing the other because of what's called interference between the two tasks. They both involve communicating via speech or the written word, so there's a lot of conflict between the two of them." (Doser, 2015)[2].

So do you need to return to the start of this chapter and read again?

Sometimes this lack of focus can be costly. One mindfulness client told me of how she took a call from her sister, expecting their usual banter about life, and so, while 'listening', she finished off composing a work email which, in her mind, she had prioritised as 'important'. She had thought, 'It's just my sister. I'll take the call. It won't be long,' and haa-ed in agreement through her sister's opening dialogue.

As a result of the brain function tuning into writing mode rather than listening she missed the devastating news that their mother was critically ill and had been rushed to hospital. Her sister was so incensed by this lack of care and attention that the accompanying stream of expletives down the line certainly woke up the client and forced her back into the auditory mode. The sisters took several weeks to repair their relationship.

Sometimes finding time to stop is about slowing down to ensure that we do one job well with focus and attention before moving on to the next.

Today's tablets and smart phones also add to life's accelerator pressure as we juggle the constant stream of information pouring into our lives. We think we've become super-efficient but in fact we've become performing monkeys.

And there is a cognitive cost in this constant neural activity because, unlike multi-tasking, the natural see-saw between focusing and daydreaming helps recalibrate and restore the brain. In other words we need to slow down and take a break.

Harvard Medical School professors, Edward Hallowell, MD, and John J. Ratey, MD, co-authors of *Delivered From Distraction: Getting the Most out of Life With Attention Deficit Disorder* (Hallowell M.D. & Ratey

M.D., 2005)[3], who have studied Attention Deficit Disorder (ADD or ADHD), have found that frequent multi-taskers may unintentionally be teaching themselves to have shorter attention spans, a condition called 'pseudo attention deficit disorder'.

Have a go at seeing if you can isolate your tasks even while reading this or during the next fifteen to thirty minutes. Perhaps say, 'I'm reading, I am drinking coffee, I am scratching my head, I am looking out of the window, I am watching the wind in the leaves, I am looking at my smart phone, I am checking the time...
During the day see if you can spot your attempts at 'multi-tasking' and check yourself. Decide which is more important and just do that task mindfully with focus. As you slow down you will find you have greater clarity and, ironically, greater efficiency as you do each task with full attention.

Our desire to speed up and its subsequent impact on our ability to focus means that concentration spans are decreasing year on year. In 2000, according to National Center for Biotechnology Information, U.S, our attention span averaged twelve seconds; by 2013 it had reduced to eight seconds (Information, 2015) [4].

Advertisers generally adopt a seven second attention span platform; in other words to grab us, whether online, TV, radio, print, or billboards, they recognise an ad has just seven seconds to do its job.

Also, according to the National Center for Biotechnology Information's number crunchers, we check our email inbox an average of thirty times an hour. Yes, please read that stat again: thirty times an hour (Information, 2015) [5].

As part of our survival mechanisms, honed as both prey and predators, we are essentially interruption-driven because we must be alert to change, says Gary Marcus, US psychologist and author of Marcus, G. (2008). *Kluge:The Haphazard Construction of the Human Mind.* New York: Houghton Mifflin Harcourt (Marcus, 2008) [6].

Scientists have also observed that once our concentration span is broken it takes between twenty to thirty minutes to refocus. Studies by Gloria Mark, a professor of informatics at the University of California at Irvine, monitored thousands of hours of workplace behaviour which demonstrated that most workers switch gear every few minutes. "When you see the hard numbers, it kind of hits home how bad it really is," says Mark. Once distracted, she has found it can take nearly half an hour to get back on track (Mark, n.d.)[7].

So that quick glance at your email inbox is proving costly in the workplace. Distractions consume as much as 28% of the average worker's day and drain US productivity to the staggering tune of $650 billion a year, according to a 2008 report by Basex, a former business research company in New York City. With the growth of email use since then the figure could have easily doubled[8].

This desire to speed up and not pay attention is not only unproductive but is detrimental to our health. Speeding up means we produce more fight or flight survival hormones, such as cortisol and adrenaline.

For a short heightened attention span to increase memory enhancement a quick spurt of energy is essential but the body then needs to return to the relaxed state of homeostasis to repair itself. If not, the long term effects of life under the cosh of these hormones is having a major impact on our health.

The chronic outcomes of stress, namely living life at speed and the constant onslaught of the speed hormones at a cellular level, is filling doctors' waiting rooms around the world.

The staggering consequences lead to higher blood pressure, suppressed thyroid functions, blood sugar imbalances, decreased bone density, decreased muscle tissue, impaired immunity and inflammatory response such as lowered resistance to colds and flu and irritable bowel syndrome, poorer cognitive (brain) performance, and, interestingly, increased abdominal fat which, combined with the modern world's poor diet of processed fat and sugar laden foods, results in higher risk of strokes and heart disease. (Pietrangelo, 2014)[9].

The call to slow down couldn't be more imperative.

Our grandparents and great-grandparents might have had it harder in that physical work was more demanding. Life without washing machines, dishwashers, vacuum cleaners, especially for the working class was perceived as a life of drudgery. It was certainly laborious; but life was spent at a slower pace. The industrialised era heralded faster transport.

Trains, planes and cars have opened up the world for us. We can get to places quicker. Modern time-saving gadgets save time.

But for us to do what with these new-found precious moments?

We are more time-free but, as I found lying under the lime tree, we have become locked in a spiral of frantic doing to fill this extra time. As we chase through our daily lists and rush from task to task the less impact we seem to make on this ever-growing schedule and so the more we think we need to be doing. It is interminable. It is exhausting.

We are also inflicting our obsessive doing-achieving culture on our children. Parents, if not rushing around to 'do' in their lives, are foot down on their children's lives, dragging them into the vortex of ballet, football, swimming, second language, painting, singing – add according to preference – then factor in school and homework, and social media, it becomes an exhausting repertoire.

No wonder child psychologists are reporting record levels of stress as kids are instilled into the go-faster, do-it-all, have-it-all, be-it-all generation. There's no down-time left for play, for developing a creative imagination which, in turn, helps evolve the plasticity of the brain and a more flexible attitude to life.

And remember, the list of physical outcomes from the over-burdened flow of 'doing' hormones will be affecting our children's bodies and mental development in the same way, if not worse.

Slowing down to play enables children to recreate and so model life around them. They learn about themselves and relationships. They develop a more holistic sense of self, of personhood, which in turn can lead to a more meaningful relationship with the world as they progress into adult life.

Arguably, all of that can also apply to us as adults. In my work as a psychotherapist I'm regularly meeting clients who've become so burnt out by their late 20's, in a bid to achieve and cram more in, that they've lost touch with who they are and with what gives their life meaning. By slowing down we develop a more holistic sense of self and a greater awareness of life around us. I will look more at this further in Step Four.

But the key is slowing down. We all want life to last. So how can we make life a marathon and not a sprint?

STEP TWO

What would it be like to stop, right now? Stop and reflect on how you can make your life slower? What would you need to jettison? What do you need to do more of? Close your eyes and perhaps remember what you had found when you did the 'When Time Stood Still' exercise?

Also tune back into your values that you considered in Step One. Aligning ourselves with our values helps us to lead a more meaningful life but also helps us become less task-orientated. We step away from rushing around to achieve our goals and discover a slower tempo.

In my retreat rose garden I reflected on my own speeded up life and realised I'd got back into a groove of not having enough time to get anywhere, not enough time to eat my food, not enough time with myself or my family. I noted that these were the key areas for attention if I wanted to slow down.

If I arrived at a meeting late would the world end? If something which I felt needed to be done was not completed that hour, that day, that week, would the sky fall in?

I now call this Chicken-Little thinking, based on the fairy tale story of the chicken who thought the sky was falling in after an acorn hit its head. In the chicken's rush to tell this news to the king it panicked all the other animals in the wood. Finally, the fox, capitalising on their stress and manic thinking, lured them to their death and so they never got to tell the king the false news that the sky was falling in.

So what kind of Chicken-Little thinking do you tell yourself? Would the sky really fall in if you didn't get a certain something done today? Do you have lists to get you through the day? Can they be streamlined? Are you over-committing?

In the main we need to prioritise better to give ourselves more time. Would you be more efficient if you just did one certain kind of task, such as organising your expenses, on one day each week or month rather than doing it in dribs and drabs between larger jobs?

As considered in Step One, practise doing one job to the very end without interruption before starting another. Try right now while you are reading this. Give yourself permission to read to the end of this chapter so a section is completed before you pick up your phone, tablet, pen, or whatever.

Part of reorganising our time means that we should end jobs and tasks earlier so we have more time to travel, whether by car or public transport. We rush because we feel we will be late; as a result we get het up in traffic which seems so much slower when we are running against the clock.

When I started my training on the eight-week mindfulness course I realised driving was one of my main stress trigger points. I love driving but was surprised how agitated I became when snarled up in traffic and the effect of this agitation on my body.

When I wasn't hurrying around to make a meeting or cram in the supermarket before racing onto something else, I drove in a chilled manner, not minding that the traffic lights were turning red, or that someone wanted to pull out from a side road. I would nod and smile at pedestrians crossing the road or even at drivers looking to cut in. I would also stop that judgemental commentary, beloved of all those in the omnipotent driving seat that everyone's driving was awful, that cyclists were not following the Highway Code by jumping the red light or that pedestrians should look before leaping out.

With a slowing down very often comes a greater sense of serenity and acceptance that things are as they are. The critical, negative, judgemental voice that comes from a position of stress is metaphorically parked. We've all driven badly, crossed a road without looking properly, cycled poorly. When we slow down we see the world, people and even ourselves in a new way because we've got time to. We find we are kinder, gentler and more compassionate to those around us, as well as to ourselves.

We'll look at the whole notion of mindful driving in the next chapter on the autopilot mode but for now consider your own driving style. Do you drive too fast? Do certain conditions make you stressed? How can you change this?

And, generally, whether by car or public transport, how can you give yourself more time to travel? What do you need to do to leave earlier? Do you really need to cram in that little extra job before you go? Instead, expect delays and plan for them. Give yourself extra time. If a journey time takes thirty minutes allow forty-five minutes instead. The extended time will also give you more time in which to be mindful!

STEP TWO

Another technique that helps reflect on our relationship with speed is walking. Week four of the Oxford style Mindfulness Based Cognitive therapy (MBCT) eight-week programme, devised by Professor Mark Williams, looks at mindful walking.

In the session you are encouraged to walk as slowly as possible from the moment of intention to walk, engaging with how the foot comes off the floor, the relationship with weight transference, through to planting the forward foot back down before picking up the other foot. Reminiscent of John Cleese in the hilarious Monty Python Ministry of Silly Walks sketch, it is an arduous but fascinating process as you connect with your agonising thoughts about being so slow.

Eventually you pick up pace until you are walking ridiculously fast. Again you watch your thoughts. Most participants love this exercise, especially those who are city-based and commute. They all recognise some aspect of their own frantic walking style in the melee of travelling to and from work, and note its relationship with the accompanying mood of stress which then becomes the default tempo of the day.

As one delegate said: "When I decided to try a new pace during my journey to the office I found a new placid mood and then a new rhythm at work. I was calmer. My team became calmer. Ironically we then won awards because we were more efficient."

Try this for yourself. If you feel stupid walking at an artificially exaggerated slow pace outside, practise indoors. Slow it right down before speeding up. Note your thoughts and emotions.

Another good tip for agitated or stressful times is to go outside and walk very fast and then slow it right down until you find a gentler pace and can use the more relaxed tempo of your body to reconnect more calmly with your thoughts and emotions.

The exaggerated state of walking is getting you out of your head with its spinning cycle of anxious thoughts and brings you back in touch with your body. This physical connection is an important aspect of mindfulness.

We spend most of the day in our heads so that over time, especially in the Western world, we've lost a sense of our bodies so that we believe we are our thoughts. We will consider this more in Step Four.

Another important aspect of slowing down is to give ourselves more time to eat. Most of us eat too fast in the West which as part of the speeding-up culture is having an impact on our health.

Eating on-the-go is a daily occurrence for most city people. Many live out of food outlets of some kind. It's called fast food for a reason. Add coffee, alcohol, and sugar and fat treats into the mix and it's a recipe for health disaster as doctor's waiting rooms around the world testify.

Spending our life as though we are prowling the savannah in fight, flight or freeze mode demands we produce stress-producing survival hormones, such as cortisol, which, in turn, correlates to reported increases in digestive related illnesses, such as irritable bowel syndrome, hiatus hernias, bloated stomach and weight gain. Other related issues to poor diet include poor sleep, concentration, and a general inability to relax.

Bolting down meals doubles your risk of being overweight according to a Japanese study at Osaka University. Its monitoring of the eating habits of 3,000 people discovered that 84% of fast-eating men were likely to be overweight. Women were twice as likely (Mark, n.d.) (Department of Social and Environmental Medicine, Graduate School of Medicine, Osaka University, Japan, Oct 2008).

This was collaborated by a study in the Journal of the American Dietetic Association (now the Academy of Nutrition and Dietetics) which found that woman aged between forty and fifty who ate the quickest were more likely to be obese than slower eaters (Barbour, 2011)[10].

Speed eating also affects the brain's off-switch which tells us when the stomach is full.

Ian McDonald, professor of metabolic physiology at UK's Nottingham University explains: "Nerves send signals to the brain that the stomach is expanding. At the same time, a hormone called ghrelin, produced when your stomach empties to trigger a hunger message, starts to decrease. It takes about twenty minutes after you start eating for the message to stop eating to reach your brain. Put simply, eat too quickly, and you're likely to overfill your stomach and overeat." (Barbour, 2011)[11].

For women the mix of living on speed, whether by activity or diet, further complicates the hormonal mix and fertility. The delicate balance between adrenaline, progesterone and oestrogen is compromised by stress and many endocrinologists are looking at the links between this and increasing reports of polycystic ovary syndrome and other conception problems. Again add coffee, alcohol and sugar into this and the problems are multiplied.

Our relationship with our food is poor. The fast food, ready-made supermarket culture means that it is a grab and go exercise. Many people haven't a clue where their food comes from or even how it is produced, as another TV dinner is added to the shopping basket, or a hot dog is grabbed at a stand.

For many all of their diet is literally manufactured, i.e. processed. They are constantly eating a collection of foodstuffs which have been chemically constructed. Reading packet labels can give you an idea of the variety of added material, usually to improve production or storage, and this all has to be processed by our digestive organs.

The impact of the industry, known as food technology, on our diets is frighteningly highlighted by the next generation. Recent research by the British Nutritional Foundation of 27,000 schoolchildren revealed that one in five of youngsters thought that fish fingers came from chicken and that pasta was from animals (British Nutrition Foundation, 2013)[12].

If youngsters don't comprehend basic food groups what hope is there for knowledge about healthy nutrition, especially as basic cooking skills are not being taught anymore.

Our inability to cook from scratch, using whole products, means we are losing vital connections with the whole food chain. This leads to a loss of value, and, more importantly, respect for what is fundamental to our existence. Without respect for what actually keeps us alive and healthy means that eating is just another part of the consumer culture, all puns intended.

As a result, we take our food for granted and regularly consume something that has little nutritional value. Slowing down to cook and eat sensibly is fundamental in nurturing and nourishing not just your body but your life.

So is it time for you to think more mindfully about how you eat? Look at your typical daily food habits. How much processed food do you have a day? How much is whole food, which means something that has not been manufactured? How often do you eat on the run? Or grab a sandwich at your desk that you absently plough into while doing something else (back to the multi-tasking misconception)?

Keeping a food diary can be quite a shock. How many coffees do you drink? And the harder question: what is your alcohol intake? Be honest - how often does that one beer after work turn into two? Or that one 'relaxing' glass of wine get refilled?

The old adage 'we are what we eat' is never so true. Perhaps we should also add 'we are how we eat'.

Wolfing down our food means we miss the experience of actually feeling the food in our mouths and taking time to savour it truly, even to a cellular level.

On one previous silent retreat in the UK I had metabolically slowed down to such a degree that eating fast became impossible. I suddenly woke up to my usual eating speed, which can only be described as inhaling my food. There was little chewing and much talking. We had always been known as a family of 'fast-eaters'. My mother would wail that she took ages to cook a meal that was over in five minutes.

Now, here I was, spaced out on silence, facing a plate of food which I would have normally have downed in a few minutes. Instead, lingering, I had to take smaller and smaller bites and longer to chew in order to be able to swallow. I was shocked. I had planned to speed through lunch so I could go off to do a meditation. I suddenly realised that the meal was the meditation.

It was a pea-pod, just one pea-pod, which turned my life around in terms of connecting with my food.

As that simple green vegetable exploded in my mouth I was connected to it cellularly. I could sense and taste all of its life juices, its essence. It felt miraculous. I could savour its life force and I felt humbled. What else was I missing if one pea pod could bring me back to life, to the beauty of food and its role in sustaining us? I ate the rest of the meal in utter reverie. I realised I had lost a sense of honour and respect for what I put in my mouth.

I started looking at my food with more interest and thinking about how it had arrived not only to this kitchen but to this town, or even this country. Our expectation in the West that food will be there, whenever and wherever we want it, any time of the day or night means we have a lack of connection with its production.

Unless we grow our own food, or cook our own meals, our separation from production means we take food for granted. We stuff it down, hungry for something else. As a result we don't value what we put in our mouths and its relationship with our physical form.

Try to eat mindfully. Find something like a carrot, apple or orange and eat it as slowly as possible. Really savour it. Make contact with the food at a cellular level. Just sit and experience the food as much as you can and note its effects on you.

At your next meal slow the whole process right down. Make it a meditation. Spend time acknowledging your food and those you with whom you are sharing. If you can't slow down or note tendencies to race it down or even binge, reflect on the thought processes that stop you from changing your eating pace. Why are you wanting to speed?

Also if you can't cook, or feel your repertoire is limited, try learning one new recipe a week. Put aside time to plan a dish, noting what you have to buy and then mindfully following the recipe instructions. This will also contribute to Step Seven – Stop Being Boring.

Mindfully enjoy your food. It's a fundamental part of enjoying life. By valuing our food we are valuing ourselves and the essential means that keep us both alive and healthy.

By slowing down we are giving ourselves a chance to learn more about our lives and ourselves. We are also improving our stress levels and their impact on our health. In the change of tempo we become more connected to what gives our lives meaning and we reconnect with our values.

Remember, it doesn't have to be a sprint. Life can be savoured and enjoyed as a marathon.

STEP THREE
Autopilot: Who's Driving the Car?
And the bird called, in response to
The unheard music, hidden in the shrubbery...

Burnt Norton, T.S. Eliot.

An outcome of rushing around and living on 'speed' is that we become hooked on our habitual routines, especially if they help streamline our daily existence and enable us to achieve our urgent sense of doing 'more'.

This is known as the autopilot in the modern day mindfulness movement and the effect of this mode is that we never really live our lives. We are simply living a version of our lives in our heads. We are either ruminating about the past or planning the near or far future. As a result we become obsessed with our thinking, to the extent that we believe we are our thoughts.

We are rarely in the here and now unless something out of the ordinary shocks us into a 'When Time Stood Still' moment. And, as we discovered in that exercise, we truly sense the impact of being alive, not just in our thoughts, but within the whole of our being.

We finally encounter ourselves and learn that we are far more than our mind: we are a complex thinking, feeling, body-sensating creature which desires to find meaning and connection in our lives.

My own example in the Introduction of driving my daughter to school, instead of the supermarket on a Saturday, dressed in my office finery, is a classic autopilot moment.

I've often wondered when my autopilot had kicked in that day. Was in it the car? Was it when I was getting ready (in view of getting dressed in my work 'uniform')? Was it even earlier when I had got up that day? Had I been stuck in my head, in the whole arc of doing, from the moment of waking?

In fact, more scarily, was I always in autopilot mode, with a few flashes of real moments?

Sadly, my conclusion was the final statement. Except for the odd jolt I was always in doing, planning, ruminating mode. From the minute I awoke the brain switched on and a day of mental activity spun into action. I'd be in continual 'thought' mode as I showered, dressed, brushed my teeth, read the paper, ate breakfast...a life of planning, in the main. In fact, when did I ever step out of autopilot mode?

By following some of the tips in the last chapter, at least when we slow down, we create time to recognise how much the autopilot function usually runs the show. We can then ask ourselves how often do we step out of our heads and truly into our life.

The best way to identify autopilot is to bring to the fore one particular routine that we take for granted and bring full attention to it.

A popular exercise in the modern mindfulness movement is to bring full sensory attention to the process of eating just one raisin from the moment it is in your hand, where you contemplate it, smell it, feel it, put it in your mouth, let it rest on your tongue and taste it, then chew it consciously through to final moment of swallowing.

Actually an ancient Zen exercise, the raisin practice powerfully brings many mindfulness first-timers fully in touch with the notion of 'being in the present moment.'

Interestingly, when I've run the same exercise in large groups many people also recognise that they are directly and immediately in touch with their senses at a very bodily level for the first time possibly since their childhood. It seems, by living in the autopilot mode in our heads, we are so engrossed in our thinking that we have lost sensory and bodily contact with our daily experience.

So choose an item of food; it doesn't have to be a raisin. It can be fruit, cheese, bread, whatever. And from the moment of choice study yourself. Forget that childhood scolding: 'don't play with your food' and play with it!

Look at the food carefully. See it for the very first time like an alien would arriving from out of space. What does it feel like in your hands? What does it smell like? If you squidged it by your ears what can you hear? Take your time with all these sensory moments. Savour them and watch at each stage: your bodily reactions, your emotions, thoughts and impulses (what you feel the urge to do).

Then when you have finished the observation period place the food to your lips and note what happens to your body, emotions, thoughts and actions. See if you can identify when the process of digestion takes places and what physical sensations that involves for you. Finally place whatever food you have chosen in your mouth and, without chewing, note again the physical, emotional and mental processes that are happening. Then slowly chew, noting everything again before the final act of swallowing.

The key aspect of this exercise is not just slowing right down but being in the present moment, watching, up close and personal, your own immediate experience. As part of this kind of exercise you are learning to 'still the mind'. Then, you can start to discriminate from what is buzzing in your head constantly to what is actually happening in your body right here and now.

Again, part of being busy and leading frenetic lives is our inability not just to slow down but to enjoy fully single moments, and yet, as we found in the 'When Time Stood Still' exercise it is our full sensory, emotional and mental connection with those fragmentary special moments that make them so memorable.

We are in touch with a greater reality, a real immediacy. We are aware that we are driving the car rather than a version of it in our heads.

There is a wonderful Zen story which brings this alive:

The disciples of two Zen masters meet one cold autumn morning on a bridge over a rushing torrent. They exchange news of their respective masters. The first says: "My master is perhaps the greatest in Japan. From one side of the river he has the ability to project his face to you on the far side so you would see him as if he were only an inch away." The second disciple replies: "That is indeed remarkable. My teacher is also a considerable master. For when he eats, he eats, and when he sleeps, he sleeps."[1]

A simple story which brings home how the state of awareness to do one task at a time requires rigid discipline.

I remember a yoga teacher once challenging us to brush our teeth with the other hand in a bid to wake us up from autopilot mode. Like the rest of the class when we returned the following session we laughed how we'd found the exercise hard, amused how we'd dribbled like children trying to get the brush awkwardly into our mouths.

And yet, every day we get up, shower, dress and eat, probably all in the same way. Lost in the space we call our minds. Lost in autopilot.

Consider some of your daily routines and try to bring full awareness to the activity. Try brushing your teeth with the other hand. Play with mindful dressing, showering, preparing meals. Take the whole activity apart and watch exactly what happens moment by moment, again, making contact with your bodily sensations, emotions, thoughts and impulses. The whole process becomes a waking meditation.

And if you really want to tackle the autopilot literally, try mindful driving – but with care. Traffic police are taught to talk through every action when driving in active situations so it can all be officially recorded. Try doing the same in your own head or out loud: "turning key clockwise in the lock with the right hand, checking the mirror…." and then when in traffic talk through the driving experience, such as, "pulling up to red traffic light, four cars away from the junction, light changing to green, going into first gear…"

You'll certainly appreciate the level of information involved with an activity like driving, all which needs to be assessed and processed by the brain, usually in fractions of a second. As well as the detail what also becomes apparent is the difficulty involved with maintaining intense concentration before the mind wanders off into thinking about something else.

When I participated in my first eight-week mindfulness course I found how much I enjoyed mindfully washing up. I had a dishwasher and could have stacked and unloaded that mindfully, but it became an absolute delight, usually in the mornings, to get up and wash by hand the breakfast items and any remaining dinner crockery from the previous evening.

Completely tuning into the activity, from the moment of turning on the hot tap and squirting in the washing-up liquid through to pulling out the soapy glasses or pans, became a fascinating meditation.

My kitchen sink overlooks my back garden so I combined the various stages with watching the wildlife. I don't think I'll call this multi-tasking, though while observing the garden I was obviously not observing the crockery.

However, I never realised how much teemed in this London suburb. The pleasure and calm I found in this peaceful, stilling experience filled my very being and continued with me for the rest of the day. Whenever I 'lost' it I could conjure the moment back up by recalling something I had noted over the suds, such as a robin on the washing line. The smile on my face would then return.

Now if I feel life is getting stressed I simply turn on the hot tap and do a bit of Zen washing-up.

Stilling the mind and just returning to the moment sounds so simple but, as you will find, it requires the utmost attention and focus of awareness. The mind likes to wander. As we discussed in the last chapter it likes to think it's busy 'doing'. Even if we are sitting still the mind will go off on some autopilot sat-nav journey of its own.

When we add the impact of living a digital life into this heady mix then our ability to be fully in touch with the whole of our experience becomes even more dislocated and distorted. Checking email, Facebook, Instagram, or any current 'in-vogue' social media platform, is so much part of the everyday experience that, as already discussed, huge chunks of our daily lives are consumed by this. Reaching out for the phone or tablet is so ingrained into our lives that it's part of the autopilot function.

On my last retreat I was intrigued by my deep resistance to switching off my phone. I was starting to think of several reasons why I should leave it on. And then caught myself. Why? I was retreating from the world, yet, interestingly, the phone was the last 'attachment' to go. So what does this device now represent to make it so interwoven into the basic fabric of our existence?

For many of us it is an attachment: our link with the outside world and relationships, the symbol of our connected self. I will consider this in more detail in Step Five concerning our meaningful relationships with others, however, here, in this context, the physical act of constantly 'checking our phone' has become a primary autopilot function.

Just become aware of your phone and tablet. Where are they now while you are reading this? How often have you stopped to check them, possibly without realising? Continuing during the rest of day and week just become aware of how often your devices pull for your attention. What would it be like to switch them off for an hour...or longer, giving yourself a break from their obsessive draw?

And if you can't switch it off ask yourself what is getting in the way? What is the fear that prevents you from being out of touch, even momentarily? What is the brain-chatter that robs you of a rare moment of complete connection with the reality of life at this very moment and this very time?

As you are probably beginning to recognise: stepping out of autopilot is an interesting discipline. Stilling the mind and giving yourself an opportunity of being 'in the moment' requires much focus and hard work.

If we keep with the autopilot car driving analogy, by bringing awareness to your autopilot functions you are giving yourself a chance to be fully in charge of how you want to drive your life.

Leading a more mindful life means that you are not living (or should that be surviving) by your automatic reactions to events, situations, people but, instead, by being more aware of your experience in the moment you can choose how you want to respond.

This brings a deeper cognitive sense to your decision processing. You are more in control rather than driving at things heedlessly or cruising through life.

STEP FOUR
Having A Meaningful Relationship With Yourself
and the pool was filled with water out of sunlight
And the lotos rose quietly, quietly...

Burnt Norton, T. S. Eliot.

Once we take on board how much we live our lives in autopilot mode and start to slow down we realise that by constantly operating in 'doing' mode we are not really living with ourselves on a daily basis. We simply don't see ourselves. We rarely give ourselves 'me' time. We take little opportunity to reflect on our lives until something seismic happens and we are forced to look at our behaviours and attitudes, often then from a deeply negative stand-point.

'Know thyself', the inscription over the ancient Greek oracle at Delphi, is a key component of living a mindful life.

Again, knowing thyself, is an extension of bringing cognitive awareness to your daily decision processing rather than knee-jerking or sleep-walking from moment to moment. It's about studying and understanding our reactions and then choosing how we want to respond. This is empowerment.

But the key question as part of this empowering process is: How much do you really know about yourself?

Already the mindfulness exercises we've considered so far have been part of this adventure and have helped us consider our habits and behaviours, many of which have become ingrained over the years. However, to know ourselves we need to find time to reconnect with our essential being, purposefully, on a daily basis.

By having a meaningful relationship with yourself, you can, in turn, have a meaningful relationship with life which logically means you can have a more meaningful relationship with others. We will look more at our external relationships in the next chapter.

This designated time to be with yourself is separate from any deliberate mindful, anti-autopilot techniques discussed in the last chapter, such as mindfully showering, dressing or even driving the car. This is about carving out a solitary time just to be with you.

For many of us these are rare moments which we accord ourselves, such as a well-earned weekly soak in the bath or lying out on a poolside lounger on the annual holiday in the sun.

Step Four is an extension of that ideal. It's simply about doing nothing, just being, at least once a day. Without phone, tablet, watch. This is not about meditation but allowing yourself to soak up just 'being'. Accept it, even if just for a few minutes, without feeling you are failing by not doing something. Or filling your precious time with something else.

This is the precious moment of being with yourself.

As a psychotherapist I have found that most of us are locked in doing mode to escape from the enormity of being with ourselves, either because we are scared of what we might find emotionally deep down inside, or because of a more profound fear of nothingness – an overwhelming innate sense of annihilation.

This in itself is a disturbing existential experience; that instead of 'being' we tap into a scary state of non-being which can lurk at the edges of our primitive 'psychotic' self.

This often equates to our relationship with death, as discussed in Step One, or is found at the heart of those rare moments in our life 'When Time Stood Still...' and what we learned in those precious seconds and minutes.

Having a meaningful relationship with yourself helps conquer some of those deep existential fears as you build up trust of resting in contemplation within a silent space and accepting yourself. In many ways it's an extension of the mindful exercises we have discussed so far.

However the difference with this step is that it's best seen as a deliberate daily placing of yourself in reflective mode; a carving out of a regular moment in the day or evening just for you.

As I said, this isn't about meditation though many involved with mindfulness use this 'me' time for that kind of reflective stillness.

This is giving yourself permission to sit on a bench in a park, in your garden, or if indoors to watch a fire, a candle, to look out of the window, or any other similar exercise which will allow you simply to do nothing but be with yourself...in silence, just for a few minutes.

Then all you do is simply notice...you.

In this connection we allow ourselves to watch a bird, smell a flower, sit and watch people go by, without reflection, comment or judgement. It's like recreating the sense of suspension in those films where the outside movement of the world is speeded up and the individual is stood still. All whirls around while the character stands serene in suspended animation.

This practice is about meeting 'you' while in suspended animation.

By creating a meaningful relationship with yourself you are finding a moment of stillness in the headlong rush of life. It is like a personal coming home.

One client told me on the back of this reflective practice that it was like being in the flow. One stands in the flow like a fisherman thigh-high in the river, hypnotically casting out the fishing line. As the river of life flows around your Being you feel at one with the forces around you. The scene feels complete, fisherman, river, fish, rod, air, wind, banks, sky, earth all in subtle unison. Eventually you realise you are not just in the flow, you are the flow.

It can be a powerful, mindful, spiritual practice.

By spending more time in this reflective state you strengthen your egoic state: that greater sense of self, outside of the masks we create to get us through our dealings with the outside world. It is about finding the innate you and giving it form and substance, and a time for expression.

The more we are comfortable and ready to sit with ourselves in a non-judgemental state the more we become ready to accept ourselves without the incessant chatter of destructive thoughts that can fuel the day: Am I good enough? Have I failed? Did I get it wrong?

In moments of personal stillness and silence we increasingly learn to park this chatter. In doing nothing but just 'being' we are giving the brain time to cool down, as discussed in Step Two – Go Slower, and find a quieter state, a slower rhythm, a re-balancing, until we rediscover an inner sense of harmony.

For me in the retreat garden at La Hublais just accepting that I could lie there on the grass and do nothing, think nothing, brought me in greater touch with my disturbed self until finally I submitted to the sensory world. I stepped out of my restless mind and into a deeper sense of self.

Suddenly I was tuning into a more powerful 'me'. I was aware of the birds, the intoxicating smell of the tiny white rosebush. I was present, fully aware, centred.

As a result I connected with some deeper meaning in me, a deeper truth about my situation. In just a few moments of 'being' I was able to alleviate my anxiety and move beyond. I was in the flow of the garden. I was the garden.

Allowing these small moments of tranquillity to flood into the fibre of ourselves can be incredibly healing.

With regular practice we learn to park the unsettled mind's desperate need when it initially settles to nit-pick at our daily dissatisfactions, and stand in this deeper flow. Often it is being alone and simply observing life around us that creates this deeper sense of almost dream-like stillness, a very different sense of consciousness.

It's a sensation of being in and out of the world that can come with that gentle liminal state before sleep, or on waking, or in the world of the lucid dream in which one dreams one is awake but is, in fact, still watching the dream.

Allowing ourselves to be caught in this reverie, without care or concern, is a subtle but powerful act of submission to a deeper self, beyond the nagging demands of the ego self which needs continually to be heard or seen.

And in this silence, this stillness, something new gets formed, like the lotus flower growing out of the mud. I like to call this suspended state the gap of potentiality. It's a fertile void where creation itself finds root; in which anything can seed, grow and find meaning.

The notion of this fertile void sits in concepts such as the primordial soup of creation and is found in most spiritual philosophies concerning the holding, non-state at the threshold of life and death such as the Buddhist concept of Bardo, the interval of consciousness between death and reincarnation.

By dropping into this deeper awareness, this sitting with nothingness, on a regular basis we are learning to accept, not just the scary unknown, but our relationship with the unknown. By having the courage to face non-existence for just a few moments of the day we are learning to trust this space at an existential level. Eventually we find that we can trust that this brief moment in space will hold us.

More importantly we start to trust what we find there: ourselves. With this holding, this trusting, comes a deeper acceptance, an acceptance of ourselves and that we can like this person, flaws and all.

A female client who was heading for a complete nervous breakdown, after suffering a series of debilitating panic attacks, found this suggested practice life-changing. Just spending a few moments with herself outside, enjoying nature and concentrating on a recommended grounding breathing technique, which I will detail in Step Eight, brought calm and serenity back into her life.

By coming back into her body and mind, trusting that these vital internal spaces could hold her fears and anxieties, she found she could heal herself.

She grew to love her daily sojourn in the garden. She started to witness the beauty and majesty of life around her and then, more profoundly, the beauty and majesty inside of her. Suddenly by developing a meaningful relationship with herself she discovered a greater healing and confidence to make the important life-decisions she had been avoiding.

The father of modern day mindfulness, Jon Kabat-Zinn, defines mindfulness as the awareness that emerges when we learn to pay attention in a particular way:

- on purpose
- in the present moment
- non-judgmentally
- to things as they are [1]

In this act we learn to accept 'things as they are' and that must include not judging or criticising ourselves. By stepping out of the cosh of the inner critic, that subtle punishing 'not good enough' voice which hounds most of our lives we find a kinder mindset that's more accepting of Kabat-Zinn's 'things as they are.'

So take time, why not here, right now at the end of this chapter, and give yourself a breather? Just take one small moment for you wherever you are reading this. Perhaps you are at home, on a train, outside. Just put the book or reading device down and sit, or, if circumstances dictate, stand.

Tune in firstly to what's happening around you. Witness yourself as though in suspended animation in a moving film. Then tune in at a deeper sensory level. If outside, feel the wind or sun on your skin, or if inside, the warmth or coolness of the air around you.

Tune into the noises of your immediate environment. Don't try to force them away. Absorb them. Become part of the sound flow.

Then visually connect with something that catches your eye. Explore it momentarily as you did with the raisin or chosen food in the autopilot exercise.

Can you smell anything? What olfactory sensations are present? Maybe you are on the way to work? Then perhaps someone's coffee cup or yours is catching your powerful smell receptors.

Now just watch all of your thoughts, emotions, body sensations, impulses. Just be with them, accepting without judgment or criticism. If the mind wanders and starts wanting to scratch at some niggling issue, tagging in your usual favourite commentary, note the issue and park it. It's not part of this exercise.

Congratulate yourself that you have noticed the mind is off doing its 'thing' and just come back to sitting or standing with a sense of yourself, reminding yourself that this is about stopping just for a few moments in silence, in reverie.

Over time you will become aware of regular thought patterns or body behaviours in different circumstances. Perhaps you find there is always one special time of the day that you enjoy this exercise? Ask yourself what that's about? What makes this a special time? Why do you give yourself permission to stop at this time of day? Why not at other times? What would it be like to change the time of your practice?

Perhaps in these moments you can take time to remind yourself of your three chosen values, that we considered in Step One, bringing them deeper into the fibre of your being and giving yourself permission to make them an active part of your life. Are you living your values right now? What needs to happen to bring them in?

Another exercise in reverie is the self-affirmation exercise called 'Who am I?' It can start with something simple such as: 'I am a man'. 'I am a woman'. Then build. 'I am a mother', 'I am a father', 'I am a daughter, a son'. 'I am an aunty, uncle.' 'I am English, American.' 'I am a teacher'. 'I am a dog-owner.' 'I am a house-owner'. 'I am loved.' 'I am lover'.

Always start with the expression; 'I am...' and allow the list to expand and flow, again without judgement or criticism. Just simply be with the many faces, statuses and essences that construct you. Note how they can change over the days, weeks, months. Ask yourself what these changes might mean for you but without any great attachment to their outcome.

If a change in 'face' or status disturbs or causes a rise in emotion just note its strong reactions but remember how many others 'faces' are still an active part of your daily life, sustaining and holding you. For instance, I find it tough to say 'I'm a daughter' since the death of my parents. I often feel sad about that but I'm strengthened by the other 'faces' I daily inhabit.

Over a period of time the 'Who am I' exercises build up powerfully to improve a sense of self-worth and awareness.

Another practice is to identify which qualities are currently operating in your life. Perhaps kick off with assessing what qualities seem innate in your being and are readily part of your essential self. You can add them to the Who Am I list. 'I am confident, I am caring, I am determined...'

Then look at the qualities that are becoming more active in your life right now. What qualities are the current conditions of your life demanding you to discover? Are you being asked to become more resilient, patient, forgiving?

And, looking forward, what qualities are still needing to be unearthed, that you aren't expressing in your life at this time?

Qualities are like seeds in the ground, some flourish naturally since birth, others grow over the years. Some might be sprouting right now and others are lying dormant, awaiting the right conditions. In the end the beauty of the human condition means that we have access to all qualities – we can be who we want to be.

So let go of those negative childhood voices that might accuse you of not being patient or giving and look how you can bring these qualities into your life. Perhaps look at your day and reflect gently on the positive qualities you represent today.

Many of us, in times of reflection, find the nagging voices of dissent and criticism overwhelming. Positive qualities can help with this. They move us on from 'ought' to 'be'. They can help us accept the day as it is.

In the end another fundamental part of the human condition is the very existential concept that whatever has happened up to today we can always turn the page and start again with a clean sheet tomorrow.

Eventually as this practice of having a daily meaningful relationship with yourself strengthens and becomes embedded in your daily existence you will find you 'know thyself' more and grow in self-worth, confidence and self-value.

What would it be like to extend this and spend an hour with yourself, or even a day just being in silence, in reverie with your very being? The growth of global spiritual retreat communities is a strong testament to the power of carving out valuable time to be with ourselves and many people openly discuss how it has changed their lives. A search online will throw up many such opportunities.

Hopefully you will now be finding, that most of the exercises we have considered so far complement and build on each other to deepen the process that we are calling mindfulness.

Whether you are treating each day as your last, going slower, stepping out of autopilot or sitting with yourself you are building a new relationship with yourself and the world around you.

However, the outcome of living mindfully is that you are sanctioning the rediscovery of meaning in your life which will overcome any destructive ideas or notions of non-being and leave you with a greater sense of self.

STEP FIVE
Having A Meaningful Relationship With Others
The surface glittered out of the heart of light
And they were behind us, reflected in the pool.
Burnt Norton, T.S. Eliot.

The next leap from spending more meaningful time with ourselves is to develop a meaningful relationship with the people in our lives, whether they are our nearest and dearest at home, friends or colleagues at work, or those people we meet during the ebb and flow of the day.

How often do we really see people in our lives? How often do we spend simple time with those around us? Often relationships fail because we are not seeing, hearing or being with the ones whom we love.

As discussed in the last chapter, much of being able to build successful relationships with others first comes from how we relate to ourselves, and, as I have learned, much of our success comes from being sensitive to the subtle fields of communication that constantly emanate from those around us.

I was powerfully brought to this realisation when I recently entered a field of horses.

This was a big moment for me as I've been nervous around horses since my early twenties when I was kicked by a moorland pony whilst eight months pregnant. Thankfully, my strong intuitive sense saved me as I ducked to miss the upending rear hoof and, instead of smashing into my bulging stomach and baby, it caught my inside right leg, resulting in severe bruising.

Upset by the animal's reaction I was shook up and traumatised by the moment but, as trauma often does, it translated into something deeper and stuck with me over the years.

This saddened me as I am an animal lover and I have worked with large animals, such as elephants and camels, which I have even ridden. However, I never really rode a horse as a child, and after the accident my interaction with horses was limited. If horses were around I didn't go into panic mode but I would avoid deliberate contact.

An opportunity to be involved in an equine therapy session, being run by a colleague, both intrigued and spooked me. So here I was in a field of horses, confronting my fear and watching my reactions.

At first I stood with the therapist, Sally, by the gate to the paddock as the two ex-polo horses, Star and Stylish trotted over to join us. Star was a wonderful, large white stallion about seven years old and Stylish, an old brown mare, nearing twenty-five years. Both were beautiful.

As Star stuck his massive head over the gate I tried to remain calm but when I looked into his massive eyes I instinctively stepped back. Fear kicked in. Would he find my gaze confrontational? Would I be too threatening? Would he bite me? I understood that all he really wanted was to know me, sense me. Instead, he tuned into my fear and, although he waited by the gate, he pulled away, as did the accompanying mare.

Sally, the equine therapist, explained that as horses are a herd animal they need to communicate instantly any perceived threats or opportunities to the rest of the herd. They attune, often silently, or through a series of noises and body language, exactly what is occurring so that the herd can protect itself to survive.

This collective communication amongst other species can be dramatically witnessed in murmurations of birds, as in a pulsing flock of starlings in flight, or in shoal balls of moving fish.

Interestingly, pack animals work together differently. The pack forms in order to harness a certain strength and pooling of skills to hunt and kill. Different communication techniques come into play to assist the pack in its mission which is one of attack as predator, rather than defence as prey, as seen in the herd mentality. The pack is more a collective of individual needs which sounds very much like western world today.

How does this hunter-hunted theme play out in society? Consumer capitalism, as the main economic construct of today's 21st century society, coupled with our notions of democracy, makes the West, arguably, a collective of individual needs.

We believe firmly in our individual rights but are my needs more important than yours? Invariably, once we find our individual needs are in opposition we are in conflict and the individual is pitched against society.

Our sense of the human 'pack animal' hunting in a team is perhaps best summed by our perception of bankers, working in the world's financial centres, under stress, to make the best 'kill' of the day.

However, as omnivores, in reality we are instinctively a mixture of pack and herd mentalities, depending on any given situation and can sometimes demonstrate herd mentalities when we are in a collective mode.

Why is all this important in developing a meaningful relationship with others?

As a therapist I've found that relationships typically break down due to a major collapse in understanding how to communicate our basic needs to each other.

What I witnessed in the paddock brought this home to me in a startling manner. As Sally and I entered the field both horses stayed at a distance to assess what we were doing. They both knew and loved Sally but were unsure of my presence and reactions. Set away from us, while we were seated under a beautiful old oak tree by the edge of the fence, I could be observed.

To my untrained eye they seemed to be just standing there, casually flicking flies off their backs with their tails but Sally pointed out the subtle signs of communication that were taking place. I was under horse surveillance.

I had noticed a horrible large equine sarcoid skin cancer on old Stylish's front left leg by the fetlock (ankle area) and the Reiki healer instinct in me wanted to direct hand healing energy towards it. As I did Stylish gradually came over towards me.

Eventually Sally and I stood to leave and I decided to brave a full encounter with these magnificent beasts. I continued to offer Stylish healing direct from my hands close to the surface of her skin but without touching.

However, Star was feeling left out and pushed her away for his own attention. He towered right up close, so I could feel his warm breath down on my face. His inquisitiveness wanted to check out the energy coming from my hands.

I've noticed when working with other animals, in particular dogs, it's as if they can see the energy in the Reiki hand and deliberately want to connect with it.

Stylish decided to stand by my left side, presenting the reddening tumour to me. I put my hands gently on her left shoulder and chest, directing energy down the leg, for several minutes until a moment came when the process became too intense, as is often the case, and the mare firmly pushed my hand away with her head.

I reconnected with my earlier fear but stallion Star quickly intervened. Pushing his huge muzzle into my hands he sucked up whatever he felt there. Amazingly, my fear was parked as this wonderful animal played inhaling and exhaling into my hands. Then he offered to lay his huge head in my palms, one side, then the other, absorbing the energy. It felt tender and majestic.

Suddenly he turned and, for want of a better description, he channelled this healing energy in the direction of Stylish. It was overpowering and deeply connecting. She stood there lifting and putting down the affected leg during the display.

Here we were – the four of us - Sally, Stylish, Star and I in the collective healing of the herd. In Star's actions I understood that by healing one, the energy was being passed around the herd. It would become a collective sharing.

This made me reflect on the power of healing the one, namely ourselves as in the previous chapter, and how that, in turn, can develop into a meaningful relationship with others.

Since my time with the horses, as a clinical psychotherapist and supervisor, I have become fascinated how my energy, when I sit with clients or supervisees, is probably passed on to families and associates and, in return, in some ether Mobius strip, how their healing energy loops and feeds back to me.

I'm certainly not claiming to be a horse-whisperer but the question now has to be: how do we tune in and relate to our 'herd' or 'pack'? Do we make enough time and give enough energy to the needs of our group, whether it is family and friends, or at work, or whatever 'grouping' in which we are involved? Do we even fully understand the needs of our group so that we can develop a meaningful relationship?

Advertising companies in the early 1970's became intrigued by the pioneering research of UCLA Professor Emeritus of Psychology, Albert Mehrabian, author of *Silent Messages*, which identified that 93% of human communication is non-verbal (Mehrabian, 1972)[1].

Call it body language or whatever, Mehrabian's research outlined that our pack-herd survival instinct means that 55% of our information is visual, namely facial, 38% auditory, by this meaning paralinguistic so the way the words are spoken, leaving just little old 7% made up of the content – namely speech and words.

For the subliminal advertiser the findings provided an invaluable tool of how to appeal to our subtle sensory language systems. However, the statistics have also intrigued researchers of all disciplines ever since.

While working with industry and organisations around the world as a communications consultant and trainer, I became fascinated by the power of non-verbal language in our relationships and how discourse is perceived and accepted.

Running crisis management training courses I noted that during examples of TV news coverage, even if the sound was muted or the programme was being aired in a foreign language, delegates could tell exactly the emotions of a presenter or corporate spokesperson. By reading the facial expressions they would recognise whether they were watching sadness, shock, grief, joy or happiness.

The same attunement is also apparent during silent group retreats. Without the usual constant onslaught of words the 93% non-verbal communication factor very quickly kicks in.

The silent 'herd' attunes to the collective emotion of the group or of individuals, sensing who is feeling down or who's struggling with something. At a glance one can read a fellow retreatant from the amassed amount of bodily information present and one becomes aware of the deeper level of communication taking place.

What does this all mean? Arguably that we are continuously emitting subtle, energetic micro-signals that we have evolved to comprehend and that there is a global human face.

Philosophers like to call this commonality of outward emotional expression the argument from analogy; namely that we can sense what someone is feeling and share that experience collectively. Of course, the greater reality is that we will never truly know if that person's experience of sadness, for example, is exactly the same as our own.

And therein lies our dilemma in communication and, more importantly, in our relationships with others. How do we bridge the gap between what is said, what is meant and what is understood? We might at a deeper level think we are reading a situation and all those micro-signals correctly, but can we be sure?

For a long time I've also been interested in whether the original Mehrabian statistics still hold true in the forty years since their first compilation and how much of our non-verbal communication skills have evolved and become more sophisticated, especially to accommodate our online-social media experiences.

The development of a range of emoticons to express various human emotions are, arguably, a testament to the pitfalls that can occur when words are stripped down to the bare 7% content in an email. Emoticons seek to re-inject the missing 55% of visual material wrapped up in the emotional content behind the written language; so please, dear reader, know that I am happy☺.

Thanks to social media sites, more and more relationships are being regularly conducted in the digital ether, in this 7% space, and, as a result, real heart connections are being lost. An energy transmission is being compromised.

For instance, I regularly used to talk to a close friend who had moved to California in the US. Our families had been close and we had shared in her starting a new life abroad on the phone, visiting her and then, latterly, online. Thanks to Facebook I knew everything she was doing on a daily basis and so felt in touch with the key events in her life, perhaps in a way I hadn't before. But we had stopped speaking on the phone.

As a result, when we picked up the phone one day and tuned into the emotional timbre of each other's voices, we realised that a deeper emotional connection had been lost and that we had been drifting apart despite the online sharing of photos, thoughts and comments that inhabit the digital space.

How many of your relationships have drifted into digital ether? Is there anyone who you feel you should call right now? Why not pick up the phone and tune into their voice again. Or go one better: arrange to meet.

The problem is that we are so busy rushing by in life we are forgetting to make real contact with people and, as a result, we are ignoring the subtle micro-signals that are an important part of forming and keeping relationships alive. We have stopped tuning in at a deeper level to read what is really going on. We have stopped meeting people.

There is little eye contact, even with those we love, there is no brief heart to heart moment, no true sense of meeting or connection. We are allowing the tiny connections to get lost and, as we now know, these micro-connections often happen without words.

So a smile or a brief eye-to-eye connection are simple but highly effective, and can change all our lives, especially in city life where connectivity seems to be more compromised.

Try this today: make a different connection with whomever you meet regularly during your daily routine, and who is not part of your immediate circle at home or work. Perhaps it's the barista at your favourite coffee shop, the official in the ticket office at your train station, someone crammed into the same tube carriage as you. Instead of ordering that coffee and going through your perfunctory routine around the purchase, make a full connection with the server. Smile, look in their eyes in friendship and wait for their eyes to make a connection back.

And then tune into the energy change. How do you feel? Has something changed? Note the subtle body signals that you can now pick up. How has the Other now chosen to respond to you? For those in service jobs it can be a faceless experience as the public comes and goes, and never 'sees' you. The person who finally 'sees' you makes all the difference. You look forward to seeing and serving them again.

What would it be like to take that experience into the workplace?

Try talking to people's eyes, using your eyes to make a real connection. You'll soon find how this is a different relationship from a 'head' connection. It's more heart centred.

Instead of emailing a colleague who's in the same office as you, walk over to their desk occasionally and make contact. What do you know about their personal lives? What would it be like to learn that the mousey woman in IT is 'into' flamenco dancing? How does that change your perception of her? How does that change your interaction with her? Would you now start to see her as someone more 'real', more substantial, than simply the mousey woman in IT?

As we found in the previous chapter's 'I am' exercise we all inhabit more than one face.

Scientists are now realising that there is more to this notion of a heart centred connection, a concept which often sits at the heart of many spiritual practices.

Neuroscientific studies are considering how all this non-verbal connection is a vital part of the brain's limbic system, a complex collection of structures either side of the thalamus area, long believed to play an essential role in our emotional development, motivation, long term memory function, as well as being connected to the 'pleasure centre' of the brain.

The evolutionary triune brain theory by the Yale University neuroscientist, Paul D. Maclean, has long held that this limbic system evolved before the forebrain to manage the fight or flight circuitry (MacLean, 1990). Some of the evolutionary aspects of Maclean's hypothesis, in terms of us having a hereditary reptilian and 'old mammalian' brain, are being challenged today but the role of the limbic system is under increasing attention[2].

This sharing of the limbic function with animals, such as with Sally's horses, is now argued to be where our non-verbal communication starts, both between humans and then inter-species, in what neuroscientists are today calling 'limbic resonance'.

In the ground-breaking book, *A General Theory of Love,* (Lewis, Amini, & Lannon, 2000) University of California psychiatry professors, Thomas Lewis, Fari Amini and Richard Lannon, argue that our central nervous systems aren't separate or self-contained but, starting in childhood, become demonstrably attuned to those around us, particularly where there's a close connection.

They call this capacity 'limbic' or 'empathic' resonance, and see it as a symphony of mutual exchange and adaptation (Lewis, Amini, & Lannon, 2000)[3].

They state that this capacity for empathy and non-verbal connection is present in all mammals, and that this shared limbic system is constantly being affected by our nearest and dearest, as we synchronize with them (limbic regulation).

Empathic resonance forms the basis of our social connections and has a profound impact on our personality, as well our lifelong emotional health. It also informs the whole healing process, as demonstrated by Sally's wonderful horses. However, when damaged or not functioning it surfaces in communication disorders such as autism and certain mental health pathologies.

This notion of collective sharing is reinforced by recent neuroscientific research which is studying the power of mirror neurons. These neurons have been shown under MRI brain mapping conditions to be involved, during moments of relationship interdependence, to mimic actions, such as copying facial expressions and other body movements.

In other words, there is a deep collective sharing of whatever emanates during these empathetic conditions which serve to keep a social group functioning and together, again as witnessed in the field with Star and Stylish.

In larger groups this has been defined as mood contagion and is, in some ways, how we mimic the collective murmuration balls of birds or fish: how one individual can impact the group and how it plays out in our ability to create meaningful relationships.

So how does mood contagion play out in our lives?

Next time you are driving and stuck in a line of traffic, with vehicles trying to join the queue from side roads, note what happens when you let someone into the line in a friendly manner. Usually other drivers will follow suit. If you do it begrudgingly, or not at all, then the atmosphere around you is not so giving and those around you are less likely to offer up a space.

Putting the car syndrome to the test I once offered a frail woman my seat on a rammed London tube. Another old man struggled on at the next station and I heard a younger guy, in his twenties, making a derogatory comment about him. So I commented that instead of passing judgement, as he was fit and healthy, perhaps he could stand and offer the disabled, older man his seat.

To be honest I was expecting an abusive reaction but the youngster stood up, slightly embarrassed and the old man took his place.

Afterwards the young man beamed to see that his gesture was copied by several others who rose to give the less able their seats. His response had been copied and, as such, validated by the herd. He really grew in stature for the rest of the journey and everyone else enjoyed the greater harmony of the giving atmosphere which we were all experiencing.

Mood contagion is like the law of reciprocation. In the above exercises niceness spreads. What would it be like to try mood contagion at work or when you are in a group outside of your home?

Firstly, using techniques we discussed in the last chapter, scan yourself and tune in to your immediate emotional experience so you have identified your own current emotional state before arriving into the work or group space. Then, when you enter, see if you can 'read' the room and sense what is happening there.

Can you tune in and name an emotion that is sitting in the environment? Does it feel happy, sad, angry? More importantly, what happens to you? As you attune can you feel yourself absorbing and adopting to the herd mood?

What would it be like to reject the mood if it's uncomfortable and negative and mindfully adopt your own more positive mindset? Perhaps sit at your desk, or somewhere suitable, and, as in the last chapter, take time to be with yourself and try emanating something different. What happens to the herd mentality now? Does your positive vibe begin to affect those around you?

Next try this at home, or whenever you are, with your closest companions. Read the group vibe. What is really happening? When you, as a family or as friends, are sitting watching TV or eating dinner together, what is being communicated by the group?

What happens if you project another emotion; what impact does that have on the group?

Again take it into your closest of relationships. If you sit in silence together what is really being transmitted between you? And how does this make you react? What is it like to look deeply into your loved ones' eyes on a more regular basis?

The key point with mood work is identifying how the group vibe not only makes you feel but, more importantly, how it makes you react. In psychotherapy-speak this reaction material is known as transference and counter-transference and, again, is part of the subtle defence mechanisms which we have constructed since childhood to make us feel safe and protected whenever our immediate environment might be under attack.

For example, your partner might have a way of sitting sometimes, distracted and silent, when coming home from work that taps into your early childhood fear of rejection. Your reaction to their moody silence might be to try to win more attention by asking questions to quell the rejection emotions which you had learned in childhood.

The trouble is you are mimicking your partner's mother's response when they were a child. She had been question-demanding and so silence was their learned defence to cope with the unease, created by the perceived aggression of the questioning environment.

So as you both become locked in your established childhood dynamics the tension will mount until it finds an outlet, either in argument or in tears, or in a deepening confused, hurt silence. These moments will continue, sometimes to the point of relationship erosion, unless both parties start to communicate authentically about what is really happening in a bid to break the pattern.

Mindfulness can teach us how to change these dynamics. By learning more about ourselves through the various exercises, we can use this growing knowledge about our reactions: physical, emotional and behavioural, so we can then *choose* how we want to respond rather than follow the well-worn path of our habitual reactions.

This is empowerment. We can choose when our well-held, early-established defences are serving us and when they are getting in the way of our own development and in the way of meaningful relationships with others.

As a psychotherapist I have found whilst working with couples and families that once the fear-dynamic is named it can understood by the various parties. It is having the confidence to identify the emotion that is sitting in the room and naming it to the herd, but, and this is the trick, without comment, judgement or criticism. It is just acknowledging and holding the herd emotion with respect.

So using the example above, if the rejected partner told his or her partner: "When someone is silent like this it reminds of me of my childhood and so I feel left out, sad, angry..." or whatever emotion is appropriate. The partner might then reply: "When I'm feeling overwhelmed I go silent so I can deal with my emotions. If I'm then constantly questioned I feel even more overwhelmed."

The key aspect in developing this style of 'holding' communication in our closest relationships is the challenge of being able to sit with your nearest and dearest's fears, concerns and emotions without comment, criticism or judgment; just simply being there.

This is empathy: you are being with someone's emotions, holding them. It is very different from sympathy, in which you are sharing emotions and so, more personally involved with your own material and issues, leading to a more co-dependent response.

Other phrases to heed during emotional sharing conversations include comments, such as 'when you say, do that, you make me feel...' Remember, no-one can make you feel anything. You can note your emotional reaction, and, as we are discovering, once we comprehend our typical reactions to given conditions we can alter these reactions and become more self-empowered to choose how to respond.

By a frank and open sharing of our emotions we are starting to build authentic relationship with ourselves and with the others in our lives.

Sometimes we are the object of someone's emotions, such as anger, and in these moments we need to help the other person work out if they are really angry with us or if it's about something else and the anger is being projected onto us.

Anger is a major signal that we are in a heightened defensive mode. It is a core survival emotion; it's the energy needed to fight in the fight, flight or freeze survival dynamics. So, as part of having a meaningful relationship with others, we need to help identify the source of the anger and separate out what's really happening.

This can be hard because anger is hot and sticky and often accusatory. It is easy to jump into the fire and meet it with more of our own fire. However, very often, the angry person simply needs to have their anger recognised. A clinical director once told me anger is either a question of not being seen or not being heard.

So think about it next time you are feeling angry. Ask yourself if you are scared about not being seen or heard in a given situation.

In conflict resolution work, whether for individuals or organisations, I have found that it is best to name the emotion you are sensing in the Other, or even in the herd. Stating to the Other something like: 'You sound angry' enables anger to find a voice and be heard, and enables the angry person to express their feelings. By having their anger validated, instead of escalation, the emotion starts to lose some of its explosive force and a greater sense of equilibrium can return, easing the conflict.

And we all want to be validated, to feel accepted by our herd, whether it is at home or in the wider community, like the young man giving up his seat on the train. We want to be seen and heard that we are doing a good job. The more we trust that our environment can 'hold' our emotions, the more confident we feel we can express them and this, in time, builds into more meaningful relationships.

As Buddhist teacher, Jack Kornfield, in *The Wise Heart* writes, echoing the musical metaphor of the "limbic resonance" in *A General Theory of Love*:

> Each time we meet another human being and honour their dignity, we help those around us. Their hearts resonate with ours in exactly the same way the strings of an unplucked violin vibrate with the sounds of a violin played nearby. (Kornfield, 2008)[4].

Part of living a mindful life is developing this capacity for empathic resonance, for our 'unplucked hearts' to vibrate with the others in our herds.

And in this wonderful resonance we are creating meaningful relationships with the people in our lives.

STEP SIX

STEP SIX
TOO MANY WASTED WORDS
My words echo
Thus, in your mind.
But to what purpose
Disturbing the dust on a bowl of rose-leaves

Burnt Norton, T.S. Eliot.

Gossip, chatter, arguments: we all waste too many words. Did we really need to say that? Was that email or text really what I meant?

We often fill the airwaves with some awful communication and live to regret the words we have chosen. How often have you sent an email and re-read it later and thought: 'OMG, did I really say that?'

When we finally incorporate the seven percent of content into our verbal communication we often speak without proper reflection.

In many ways this chapter is an extension of developing meaningful relationships with others and not living in autopilot mode. It is furthering our sense of communication by understanding the old Buddhist adage from the Dhammapada scriptures: 'Better than a thousand useless words is one single word that gives peace.'

During my retreat in France I learned this the hard way. Having spent five days in silence and enjoying the 93% non-verbal communication as a deeper group 'holding', it is always interesting to look at why we break the silence during the retreat and what we choose to say when we are first able to find our voice again.

In a given moment of silence-breaking I deeply regretted something I'd said to a colleague with whom I was working, and, as with all retreats, whatever happens feels one thousand times more amplified than in 'real' life.

During the retreat our guide, who spoke throughout to facilitate the process, asked us to team up with someone and tune into them, in a similar way to how we worked in the last chapter. I didn't know any of my fellow retreatants and had regularly sat next to a woman called Joy who

56

played the music during the retreat. I had enjoyed singing with her, the only time we were supposed to be using words out loud.

As I tuned into Joy I found something that I had sensed during the time seated together: a solidity and determined sense of self, combined with a deep love of giving and sharing. When we came to the moment when we were being asked to share what we had intuited she reflected back something of real warmth about me and I felt bathed in her kindness.

When it was my turn I struggled to find the right word for what I was sensing and instead of taking my time and reflecting more deeply on the impact of my words, within the deeper crucible of retreat life, I blurted out something about stubbornness and a wonderful sense of self.

Out of context 'stubborn' was a word of hurt and was not what I had meant. I can make all sorts of excuses but, in effect, I had been thoughtless.

Thankfully she was wise enough to reflect back that she wasn't happy about this observation and that there could be a more positive way of summarising this quality if I took my time. I made a pathetic attempt to justify myself which worsened the exchange.

Again the intense nature of retreats made the whole emotional journey around this moment deeply painful. I was embarrassed and felt a clumsy clot. I couldn't believe after all my work as a psychotherapist I could have been so insensitive. Words were my stock in trade from my years previous as a journalist and communications consultant, and now part of the healing process in my therapeutic practice space.

Being stubborn in my family is a note of praise and a sign of strength – something to be celebrated but I hadn't stepped into Joy's shoes and thought more about how someone else might receive my hasty words. I had stumbled in.

How could my first spoken words been so crass? How I had not relished the power of the word and chosen with more care?

During the rest of the retreat I constantly replayed the scene in my mind, wishing I could have done it so differently. As we were confined back to silence, I couldn't fill the air with more and more words to apologise and I was left with my growing sense of shame.

I recalled another retreat when the silence was finally broken by the traditional 'welcome back to the world' meal of fellowship; then a

57

colleague had told a really crude story, full of swearing and risqué innuendo. It was all too inappropriate for the gentleness of the herd's mindset, re-entering after its collective time out together in space. Many of the group were appalled.

For the swearing retreatant it was almost the antidote for the holiness of the retreat and perhaps the rest of us had needed, on a deeper level, to be jolted back into the mire of the world.

However, my bumbling at La Hublais made me realise the enormous waste of some things that are uttered.

In this case I was fortunate that Joy was mature enough to feed back the impact of what I had said. At the end of the retreat we hugged and I took her to a beautiful tree where I explained how I found her like this tree, rooted and beautifully centred, yet with the flowing, swaying nature of its branches, to be giving.

She was a joy – and had certainly been very 'giving' to me but it could have been very different. Another person could have harboured my ill-chosen words in shock or pain.

Very often we never know the impact of our words – good or bad. Usually we say far too much, especially in the heat of the moment. Learning to step back, bite our tongue and take our time to choose our words with care is an interesting test of patience and a study in our relationship with words.

While writing this, I keep thinking of the line from the Bible 'In the beginning was the Word'. Many see this statement as Word as *logos*, with the inherent meaning of knowledge encapsulated in the ancient Greek concept of logos, but also Word as sound, the divine resonance which provided the energy of creation.

Word as resonance takes us back to the notion of limbic and empathetic resonance, considered in the last chapter. Often it is not just the word itself but its tone and resonance that can affect us, for good or bad.

I see many clients who still suffer deeply from the names they were called in childhood, either by bullies at school or at home. The old adage 'sticks and stones can break my bones, but names can never hurt me' is blatantly untrue. The resonance of words, whether kind or unkind, vibrates deep in our core and can last a lifetime.

Comprehending the power of resonance as healing is an important aspect of some retreat work. It is explored through music with its impact being felt even more profoundly as it stands in contrast to the silence for rest of the time.

Sound is a fundamental cornerstone of the major spiritual practices and religions from the Ohm of Buddhism, the wasaif of the Sufis, to the Santa Maria of the Catholic faith.

Religious or not, we have all felt the power of a particular song or piece of music that has touched us emotionally and has changed our lives in some ways.

Recall a piece of music that makes you feel sad with memories attached or another that brings joy to your heart. Perhaps play the pieces now and note which part of your body responds to the sounds and sit with the emotions that lie there. Feel the resonance inside of you.

When the music is finished sit in the silence and note how the soundwaves continue their work in and around you. What part of you is the 'unplucked heart' that is resonating? Is there a part of your body that is responding to the after-sounds? What is it feeling? If it had a voice what would it be saying to you?

The power of sound is explored today with healing practices such as sound bath therapy. Sound therapists use a mixture of instruments, such as the expanding resonance of Tibetan singing bowls, to create the healing waves.

Words carry the same weight; they can heal as well as hurt. The trouble is that we so often speak without really listening that we forget to tune into the wisdom of our herd.

So let's be more pro-active and start listening hard, not just hearing, to what is actually being said by ourselves and those in our life.

Watch your daily discourse with those around you at home, out in the world and at work. Note how often you use the same phrases and how much of conversation is routine. Do you like what you say? Do these phrases serve a real function?

Often we use words at home and in the wider world as ritual. They are an important part of social interaction, therefore communication, with our herd. Certain phrases signify social functions like codes.

For instance, count how many times you say 'thank you' while buying something at the till, especially if you're based in the UK. Someone once did a video for TV and counted at least ten exchanges of gratitude as part of the 'buying contract' in the UK. Foreign visitors find the behaviour confusing and often hysterical, and, like much coded, cultural behaviour, very hard to mimic at the start unless you've lived in a country for a long time.

Watch your own behaviour during your next shopping exchange at the till, wherever you live in the world, and see if you can identify the codes that sit behind this contractual moment.

In the workplace a variety of languages proliferate to denote that we belong to a particular working 'herd'. Each industry equates to a community of interest with its own phraseology. Examples include the obvious, such as medical world language, technical IT speak, political speak. As a member of that tribe or herd you can tell instantly if someone really belongs to the group by whether they know the right language or not.

As a therapist we have the 'space', the 'container' for where we meet 'clients', which in some situations and countries are called 'patients'. We talk about 'attachments' and 'disassociation' and 'dynamics'. Wherever I am, I know when I'm talking to another therapist, even if we are meeting for the first time. This is language as code, or secret password; that we share some form of herd identity and that we can feel safe in this bonding.

Think about the language of your working group. Listen to the words that might not have real meaning or a very different meaning in the everyday speak of the wider world you live in.

The next part of the exercise is to assess how much of the daily discourse involves dead words, namely words that have no meaning. How many of these words are so meaningless that they are not understood by much of the herd but are simply repeated so the member can appear to belong?

A good example of the last exercise is the collapse of the global banking business in 2008 and onwards, relating to the US sub-prime mortgage fiasco. The financial language that had grown up around this bond industry was obscure and complex. Later, the exiting chairman of the then collapsing Royal Bank of Scotland, Sir Fred Goodwin, admitted he hadn't fully understood what the advisors were talking about.

As a leader of a major bank not to grasp the implications of what was really lurking in the detail was later judged to be inexcusable but in many ways this is words as Emperor's New Clothes. None of the crowd dare point out that the emperor is not wearing anything, namely that the words don't make sense, until the young boy shouts out the obvious: 'the emperor has no clothes.'

Imagine if just one of the leaders of the banking industries had played the ingenuous boy the world might not have headed into the financial abyss that haunted the end of the Noughties.

While working in communications I would often ask the simple question, when faced with verbosity or inflated language; 'what do you mean?' As a journalist I had learned that if I was going to write or broadcast a piece, the onus was on me to translate the language of the different communities of interest into everyday speak, the domain of general media. So I had to ensure the expert I was interviewing could explain in language that they would use with their friends in the pub.

'What do you mean?' usually proves to be a devastating question and can quickly reveal those who really understand what they saying and those who are dangerously repeating the industry in-speak so they appear to belong. As Einstein is often quoted as saying: 'If you can't say it simply, you don't understand it well enough.'

Admittedly, it takes confidence to state that you don't understand what someone of your herd is saying which is why so many just go along for the ride, but long-term bluffing can be costly or even dangerous, depending on your job. If you have to take responsibility for the outcome of any given event or words, it's best to make sure you understand what you are signing up for.

The more you choose to listen before speaking, the more you find you will also tune into the 93 percent non-verbal language we discussed in the last chapter, and the more you will develop meaningful relationships with those around you.

As at work, families also have an evolving language only relevant or comprehensible to those in the group. Catchphrases, shared imagery or jokes and routine phrases, particularly those around mealtimes such as 'grub up' or 'on the table', all serve to create the vital group bonding.

So note what language is typically used in your home for everyday interactions. How do you feel about these phrases? How do they make you react? How do they serve your family group? When is language fun and why? When does it become more formal? What words does your family usually choose for banter and what words for conflict and its resolution?

Does one person speak more often than others? Is there someone who rarely has a voice in family matters? What would it be like to include them?

This can, of course, apply across your community spectrum of groups. By listening you will learn much more about the linguistic ebb and flow of your group.

Another consideration is not only regular phrases and words that make up your daily banter but the whole package called opinion. How often are you offering your advice, opinions, judgements and criticisms throughout the day, whether at work or home or with friends?

Try holding back when in a group or one to one. Let people talk and resist any desire to comment or offer opinion. What happens when you're silent? How does the family, or group, dynamic change? Would your opinion have served any function? Do other people's opinions contribute anything significant or a deeper meaning?

As Sufi master, Hazrat Inayat Khan, wrote: 'Wisdom is not in words, it is in understanding. If there is no understanding between two people, words are of no use.' [1]

Keeping your opinion to yourself or simply practising the exercise of saying less is powerful. Control over your words leads to greater willpower and control in other aspects of your life.

Another check is on your choice of words, especially when you feel the need to swear. Obviously there is a link with swearing as an expression of anger, but language has evolved, especially in recent times, so that expletives can be a venting of surprise, admiration and even happiness. 'What the F**k, who'd have known??'

Psychologists are discovering that swearing is another part of the fight or flight defence mechanism we've considered in earlier chapters; in this case foul language possibly contributes to relieving pain.

A study published in the journal, *Neuroreport* found that participants, when asked to keep their hands in freezing water, could endure the temperature longer if they swore. Swearing increases heart rate, a key feature of the survival mechanism, which in turn makes us less sensitive to pain (Stephens, Atkins, & Kingston, 2009)[2].

Studies have also shown that, whereas normal language involves the outer millimetres in the left hemisphere of the brain, a good cursing relies on those evolutionary survival functions deep inside the right half region. WTF?!

However, before you get carried away with the *??!!* the Keele University team in the UK, behind the report, also discovered that the more people swear the less potency the words offer as pain relief (Stephens, Atkins, & Kingston, 2009).

So how many swear words are you wasting? Check how many times you swear. Tune into the occasions for swearing. How often is it an expression of anger, or something else? Do you like the sound of these words? Are they necessary? Has swearing become excessive? Try a day or longer without swearing? Note the control this can also give you over other aspects of your daily discourse.

Part of your exploration with words is the opportunity to explore silence. For many people with public/customer focusing jobs, coming home and then being instantly involved with family chatter is exhausting.

The tongue is possibly the most over-used organ, a former yoga teacher would say; so reward yourself with silent breaks during the day.

STEP SIX

This is definitely an extension of creating meaningful moments with yourself that we discussed in chapter four.

As Baba Ram Dass, the American spiritual teacher, states: 'The quieter you become, the more you can hear'[3].

STEP SEVEN
DO SOMETHING DIFFERENT EVERYDAY
Go, said the bird, for the leaves were full of children,
Hidden excitedly, containing laughter.

Burnt Norton, T.S. Eliot.

We are boring! We get up and generally live our life in a set groove, until we go on holiday and then we might briefly venture out of our comfort zone. We simply forget to play. We forget to act like a child and explore life anew with fresh eyes.

Some Daoists say the reason we age is just that: we lose our inherent child-like ability to find the new in every moment so the moments rush by.

During the La Hublais retreat I watched those around me worried about getting soaked in the rain on the way to lunch, and thought: 'why are we cowering in this porch?' We didn't have to sit around in wet clothes all day, catching a chill. It wasn't hazardous. We were locked in a parental, finger-wagging mindset that encouraged us to worry rather than to play.

Instead of being in the moment and thinking: 'what the heck if I get wet?' we were going down the prescribed path of what was expected of us in any given situation. It made me question how often the parental, censoring voice which we learn in childhood now blocks us from enjoying the simple pleasures in life.

So on retreat I decided to skip in the rain. I took off my shoes and felt the sodden ground beneath my feet. When I woke up at night, instead of fretting about not getting enough sleep, I gazed at a stunning crescent moon and was rewarded by seeing a deer.

Even now I can recall both moments on every sensual level. I can still feel the wetness oozing between my toes. I can still see the face of the startled deer. Instead of day merging into day they have become significant moments. They have transcended time and now come readily to mind. Their emotional and sensory content mean they have become

65

easily accessible memories, rather than getting lost in the deep archival recesses of my mind.

By doing something different, I managed to make an ordinary moment, extraordinary. Another day is imbibed with a larger dose of meaning so that I had the opportunity to expand my sense of self rather than get lost in the routine of my life and limiting myself.

As Marcel Proust states: 'The real voyage of discovery consists not in seeking new landscapes, but in having new eyes.' (Proust, 2006)[1].

These concepts are an extension of Step One, *Treat Each Day as Your Last,* and Step three on Autopilot. However, as we come to the final chapters I hope you are beginning to realise that this is about adopting different mindsets which will help you create the framework to discover a more mindful, happier and meaningful life.

Inevitably, the set groove of routine is an important structure in our lives. Our existence and sense of self is held in place by our relationship with the structures of time and space and purpose.

We get up and eat; we go to work to earn money to survive; we have daily domestic arrangements and family commitments, such as taking the kids to and from school at a set time, or going to the gym on the same evenings each week. We have daily, weekly, monthly and annual rhythms and patterns of behaviour.

These repetitions are often essential containers and help us feel rooted and grounded in this world; but they do not serve us if we allow them to stagnate and hold back our growth.

Many of these routines are so instilled they operate at an unconscious level, almost like the automatic reaction of breathing. In and out, we live our day which merges into weeks, months and then years, to the point that we start living our whole life on autopilot.

Arguably, we are not living; we are existing until something momentous comes along, such as the death of a loved one, divorce, redundancy, to shake us out of our complacency and force us into change.

If our lives have been very rigid and shut down then this kind of change is overwhelming. We often haven't learned the tools to cope and the shock drives us to our doctor, and the arms of the pharmaceutical industry in the form of anti-depressants.

However, change is constantly all around us. Many of us fear the unknown rather than dare stand in its flow and embrace whatever comes our way. As we've discussed earlier, this touches our death instinct and, as a result, it takes faith to let go and trust all will be well.

A mindful life helps us to develop this kind of trust. By learning to accept the present we lose our steely grip on wanting to control the future.

Whether we are accepting, or not, life is series of beginnings and endings, however minute, so it means all of us are constantly having to handle change.

I will consider how we handle beginnings and endings more in chapter nine, but what would it be like to introduce change deliberately into your life to build a better relationship with it? What would it mean to shake yourself up every day? How could you approach each day anew in a childlike fashion?

Let's start simply by making a conscious effort to do something different every day. Choose something small but deliberate.

Remember to try brushing your teeth with the other hand, always fun and also a popular anti-autopilot exercise.

Have something different for breakfast, lunch, dinner every day, especially if you're someone who gets stuck in a routine with food.

Buy your coffee or groceries from another store.

Come home a different way.

Watch a different TV programme.

As we discussed in Step Three try switching off your mobile or tablet for an hour, several hours, the whole day. How does that make a difference? And again as in Step Four, 'Having a Meaningful Relationship With Yourself', what do you find in the silence? Can you cope with not being connected but in the unknown?

Most of these moments are about deliberately challenging yourself to study the routine of your daily life and your behaviours, and shake them up.

On a weekly basis look at what becomes rigid for you. Admittedly it's hard to change your routine when you're going back and forth to your usual workplace but there are always small chinks that offer up a new creative approach.

I really like a colleague's wonderful impulsive act of selecting a day in the week to go to the cinema at 7pm and see whatever film is showing. She doesn't book. She doesn't choose before she leaves. She just turns up and decides there and then.

As a result she has seen masses of movies which she would normally never have viewed. She has expanded her knowledge of film but, more importantly, she has not settled her mind into that well-worn groove of what she thinks she likes and dislikes. It has been liberating for her.

On a similar note, a cameraman friend adopts this approach to weekend travel. When the dirt cheap deals come up on airlines like Easyjet or Ryanair in Europe he buys the cheap tickets to destinations he's never visited and books out the weekends throughout the year. If he finds he can't make the booking because of other commitments there's no real problem because he's only lost a £15-£20 cheap air-ticket but, usually, he takes up the trip as he's already factored it into his plans.

Again, he's visited obscure places he'd have never seen. He's deliberately doing something different.

It reminds me of the poignant poem by Mary Oliver, *When Death Comes,* she concludes:

When it's over, I don't want to wonder

If I've made of my life something particular, and real...

I don't want to end up simply having visited this world (Oliver, 2004)[2].

So, look at your week, your month and think about what you can change. Think of this as fun, as a creative way of living your life. Think of this as play, as waking yourself up, rather than just visiting this world!

In the workplace leadership gurus usually state that the definition of a good manager is someone who can lead their team through change and show them how to cope. So how are you dealing with change at work?

If you are a manager study how you are managing change for your team. How do you introduce change? How do you bring creativity and difference into the workplace? Do you encourage staff to change and adopt new practices or learn new skills?

Whether you work, or not, how often do you resist getting to grips with the latest technological developments for fear of getting it wrong or are scared of facing the frustration technology know-how can encompass? The computer-digital world is constantly upgrading and it's easy to get left behind. So what new function or package could you be learning or downloading now?

Then what about embracing difference on a bigger scale? The dreaded New Year resolutions, usually abandoned by the second week of January, can become objects of fun and creativity. Instead of thinking about losing weight or drinking less, both of which are quite admirable of course, what about stepping outside of the box and going for something you've always wanted to do.

Often we reserve these 'in my dreams' accomplishments for a proposed 'year out', or even for the presumed end of our working life, our retirement. Sadly, we probably all know someone who promised themselves a particular adventure or new hobby for those halcyon years beyond age sixty or sixty-five but who died suddenly just before or after the golden retirement date.

The moral is simple: If there's something you dream of doing – get on with it!

Try learning something or doing something new each year. And don't feel you have to wait until the start of the year if you're reading this half way through, in June, July, August, for example; do it now.

This year I've taken up Tai Chi again. Next year I'm planning to take singing lessons. I can hear my family groaning already but it's something I've always dreamed of doing, so why not?

So what's on your 'bucket list'? What can you start today - a new sport, hobby, language?

Another interesting exercise is to record each unique moment that you have lived each day of the year. I spent one Christmas and New Year with family in Vancouver, Canada, and, avid skiers, we rented out an apartment up in the nearby ski resort, Whistler. The weather was cold and the daily programme of exercise on the ski slopes challenging.

STEP SEVEN

Instead of going out for the resort's New Year's Eve firework spectacular and skiing displays, once we had got back and changed, the warmth hit us; so feeling tired, some of us agreed to stay in.

I regretted it immediately. What was I doing? This was a unique moment. Back to Step one: Was I treating each day as my last? No. I might never come back to Whistler. I was missing a very different experience.

Incredulous, I vowed I'd never repeat that mistake. Taking a calendar that a friend had given as a Christmas present, starting with January 1st I wrote in each daily box for the whole year something unique that I had done that day.

The exercise was enlightening. It helped me note my regular patterns and behaviours. It made the special moments jump out. I had to work on days that were repetitive to incorporate something I'd never done in my life such as deliberately buying food I'd never eaten or walking a different route.

Each day, sitting down with the calendar, become a secret joy. Each day became an adventure as I felt the pull of curiosity about what was truly unique in my life, despite having been on this earth for 50+ years.

Little moments when I flick through the year still make me smile, such as eating Cheshire cheese with cranberries and blueberries, doing a jigsaw puzzle with a friend, buying an orchid for my new office, meditating during a full eclipse. Little moments of magic scattered through the year, alongside some of the bigger moments: sad death of a friend, holidaying in Sardinia, buying a new car with my partner.

Doing something different every day brings you back in touch with curiosity and your own creativity. In daring to push the boundaries of change you are reconnecting with the unknown and developing an attitude of healthy enquiry, rather than being stuck in old fear based patterns.

Subtle and persistent, this approach can eat away at old attitudes and beliefs. It gradually builds into a new joyful way of looking at life as you embrace the possibility of the unique still waiting for you in your daily life, however old you are.

So challenge yourself. If you don't like the tedium or boredom of your life – change! Even if it's only something small - wake yourself up.

STEP EIGHT
KNOW YOUR BREATH
Disturbing the dust on a bowl of rose-leaves
Burnt Norton, T. S. Eliot.

Breath is life. Constantly there, in the background providing the life force. Breathing in, breathing out. It is the pattern of our life from the minute we take our first gasp to the final sigh out.

Understood by yogis, ancients, and spiritual adepts, it has been explored from the early Egyptians with their images of the ankh – the handled cross (crux ansata) symbol of the breath of life - being placed inside the human by the Goddess Isis, through to images of the Christian Cross.

The notion of the fertile gap, the void in which resides all possibility, sits within the context of the breath. As we breathe in and out we are usually unaware of the little pause between each part of this essential automatic reflex – but pay attention and there it will sit, gently keeping the beat, a vital part of the rhythm of the flow. The Daoists believe it's the breath within the breath.

How much is our breath part of a bigger symbolic patterning: as the earth breathes in each day after the pause of daybreak and breathes out again at night after the gap at sunset. Or again breathes in after the gap at the Winter solstice and breathes out after the Summer solstice each year.

Are we part of a greater breathing organism called the universe; a simple cell in a collective respiration?

Many ancient breathing exercises play with both the breath and the pause, inhaling in different manners for different counts in and out, and holding the pause for varying stated periods. Adepts will tell you that these exercises can promote different health and physical benefits.

In this chapter we too are going to pay closer attention to this fundamental aspect of life and consider how our breath can be a barometer of how we are feeling. We will look at some simple breathing exercises. If you are interested in exploring this in more depth then an online search will produce numerous videos to follow or groups for you to join, whether they be meditation or yoga classes.

As in previous chapters, let's start by looking at your relationship with your breath. This can be incredibly revealing from the minute you get up through to eating breakfast, running for the bus or train, sitting down or climbing up and down the stairs. The breath is constantly changing its rhythm during the day.

Notice how it changes from moment to moment, day to day, week to week, and so forth. It will be an indicator to your mood, your hopes, fears, your well-being. It is the physical aspect of you. By having a better relationship with this wonderful automatic process you will find a better way of knowing yourself.

Watching the breath is also a pre-cursor, and then anchor, to successful meditation but, as stated at the start of this book, you don't have to meditate to be aware of this essential life force keeping you alive.

So let's analyse what happens for you during a typical day. From when you wake watch the breath getting out of bed, while running for the bus, working out at the gym or watching TV. Notice when your breath is pounding in your chest or when it is small in your throat.

First of all, just check right now where your breath is 'entering' the body. Sit, or stand, and find out where the journey starts: is it at the nose, the mouth, in the throat, chest or starting deeper down in the abdomen?

Just follow the breath in and out. See if you can stay with the breath. A good way to do this is to feel it coming into the nostrils cold and out warm. Are you breathing shortly in the throat area or more deeply from the lower abdomen?

As you sit with the breath what happens? Does it slow down or speed up when you bring your attention to the process?

Can you start to play with your breath?

See if you can keep it at the nose for several breaths. First breathe in through both nostrils and then alternate between the left and right nostril. Eventually start taking the breath down on a journey – breathing in at all the regions mentioned: nostrils, throat, chest, deep abdomen.

Is any region harder than another to breathe from? Perhaps explore that by breathing into the tightness and note what emotions, thoughts, ideas and sensations surface.

By breathing deeper into an area we can explore aspects of our lives that are sitting there, that we are holding onto. Sometimes we feel a tightness in a part of the body, say in the neck; by breathing there we can ask our self what that might be about. By using the breath to soften and open a tightness or bracing or niggling pain, we can often unlock something deeper onto which we are holding psychologically.

The assessment breath can be an amazing release mechanism and a vital healing tool.

Under the lime tree on retreat I noticed how my breath settled deeper, further down into my abdomen, once I had connected with the shorter breathing in my upper chest which was related to my rising levels of anxiety. Contacting this lower breath and working with it, without forcing it, but just accepting its slower, deeper rhythm helped then to produce a calming, peaceful state.

As I dropped into the slower, deeper breathing pattern I felt I was dropping into a deeper space, more in tune with nature around me. I was breathing with the garden. It felt deliciously harmonious and in sync. It was deeply healing.

And this is the power of working with the breath. This kind of connection is an important aspect of preparing for meditation but it can be useful at any time of the day. It is certainly always on tap and available, though those who suffer from panic attacks, or deep anxiety, will know, at these times the breath can feel in short supply. I will look at this further later in the chapter.

By paying attention to the breath we start to notice and evaluate its qualities. Is it weak, strong, urgent, calm? Where do these different breath qualities live in the body? For instance does the urgent breath live in your upper chest or throat? When you're calm is the breath deeper down in the stomach/abdomen region?

In this exploration you can analyse the pattern of the breath to that of your moods. How do they match? If you're tense do you find that your breathing is shallow, sitting tight in your throat?

The power of this relationship is that over time you can tune into the breath, perhaps noting that it's in the region you associate with being stressed and then moderate this feeling by using your calm breath to alleviate any stress-based symptoms.

An interesting aspect of this work is tracking the breath during the day to see what influencing factors might have a bearing on your respiration and your overall well-being, whether they are physical or emotional.

Start a breath diary so you can compare how your breath changes over the course of your typical day. It's easier if you set your alarm at certain times of the day for a planned breath check-in. How and where is your breath at breakfast, lunch, dinner, for instance? How is it when you walk into work and then when you leave?

If you use one of the body monitoring devices you can then compare these notes with the daily read-outs to provide extra valuable information about your physical make-up.

How is your breath when you exercise? Are there times when it is higher in the throat or sometimes when you start exercise do you note it's calmer and lower down, meaning that your ability to exercise is greater than when the breath is in urgent mode?

Many professional sportspeople have found that their warm-up to kick start training or in preparation to engage in the sport itself, not only tones the body and prepares the muscles but stabilises and moderates the breath so that it is balanced and even. At this point the body and mind are at full effectivity.

The healing aspect of the breath also works in many ways. On a simple day-to-day level breathing into painful, or tight regions is highly beneficial. As discussed, both the focus of attention and the concentration of breath can often release something.

I often like to work with colour visualisation, using the accepted chakra colours appropriated to the site of pain. So if I've got a cold or my chest is tight, I will breathe into the chest region visualising green, the colour associated with the heart chakra. I will sit quietly, breathing the colour deeply for several minutes, whether I'm at home, travelling or at work.

STEP EIGHT

The main chakra colours are: red for the base chakra at the bottom of the spine, orange for the sacral chakra, the region around the reproductive organs and below the naval, yellow for the stomach and solar plexus region, green for the chest and heart, sky blue for the throat, indigo blue for the third eye (centre of the forehead) and mauve/purple for the crown, just above the head, useful for those with headaches or general malaise.

A good daily breath work-out is to work with all the chakras and clean your aura.

So sit on the floor, or in a chair, with both feet flat on the floor to 'ground' you. This is important. If you are sitting in a chair spend some time allowing your breath to settle by feeling the chair around you, conscious of it supporting your legs, bum, back, arms. If you are on the floor be aware of the ground supporting your weight. Then breathe in and out three times. If you like, in through the nose and sighing out through the mouth. The outward sighing breath is a great way of releasing stress and physical tension.

Now imagine you have roots extending from your feet deep down into the earth. Allow them to anchor into the life force energy of this planet before then breathing it up your roots, through all your chakras, pausing at each one to allow its colour to be charged by the energy. If you like, you can see each chakra as a ball of colour that is set into spin motion by the earth's rising energy.

So base – red, sacral – orange, solar plexus – yellow, heart – green, throat – blue, third eye – indigo blue, crown – purple.

Then as the energy passes through the crown chakra see it become a white light made up of all colours that then flows down into the aura of light that surrounds your own body like a protective cloak. Visualise this powerful white light energy as repairing and strengthening your cloak, as it washes away any negativity back into the ground where it is restored into the positive life force.

This is a powerful visualisation that can be incorporated into any daily routine, whether at the start or end of day, or before or after exercise.

As well as working with colour energy as a restorative and healing function, we can also use the elements in the same way.

Like chakra breathing, elemental breathing is at the heart of many ancient spiritual practices. By tuning into the four elements of earth, fire, water and air which also have correlations in the body, we can feel re-energised and balanced.

Ideally, the practice is best done outdoors, whatever the time of year. I love donning my coat first thing in the morning and doing these simple breathing practices in my winter garden. Even though I live in the city it helps me tune into Mother Nature and the natural rhythm of life around me.

The exercise is empowering and connects you with your new found mindful approach to life at the start of the day, getting you into the right frame of mind. If you can't go outside, don't worry as you can still do this anywhere, preferably standing.

So the earth breath is simply breathing in and out of the nose. As you start the process flex your hands at the wrist as though you are drawing up the earth' energy through your palms. Imagine you are contacting the earth and its strong magnetic force in your mind's eye. Feel it strongly beneath your feet and simply breathe it in.

You can do this for as little as five breaths or longer, depending on your inclination and available time.

The next breath is the water breath. For this you are tuning into water as the all-powerful element that is fundamental to life. We are predominantly water - it makes up 75% of adult body weight, with 70% of our brains water and 90% of our lungs. More than 70% of the world is covered in water. So our connection with water is essential.

The water breath involves breathing in through the nose and out of the mouth. As you breath in through the nose visualise you are wading in a beautiful clear stream to a waterfall; as you breath out of your mouth imagine the waterfall cascading gently over your body, its flow caressing your skin and bringing you back in harmony with this vital element.

Again you can do this for as little as five breaths or longer, depending on your inclination and available time.

The fire breath is centred in your heart and is the breath of the assertive force associated with fire that can power through anything. For this breath you breathe in through the mouth and out of the nose. As you breathe in imagine a fire whose coals start to glow with the passing air; as you breathe out put your hand to your heart and visualise the flames from the coals beginning to dance. You can then visualise the fire energy of your heart pouring out of all of your sides to the universe.

If you have a cold or chest problems this can be a very healing breath. If you lack energy, or need to find more empowerment for the day, this is also a good engine stoker.

Again do this for as little as five breaths or longer, depending on your inclination and available time.

The air breath is breathing in and out of the mouth. As you know we need air, i.e oxygen, to survive. Like water it is fundamental to life. A good visualisation for this element is to imagine when breathing in through the mouth that there is a pile of leaves above your head, as though these leaves are all the thoughts and ideas that are cluttering your mind. Then with the out breath imagine these thought-leaves are being blown by the wind to the four corners of the world, freeing up your mental space.

Again do this for as little as five breaths or longer, depending on your inclination and available time.

As with all breath exercises regular practice will highlight variabilities and patterns. Do you have an affinity with one element in particular whose practice is easier than the others, for instance? Are you a more earth, water, fire or air person? Are there any blocks with one element registering an uncomfortable breath? Pay attention and use the breath to explore what that might be about.

Elemental psychology was a preferred personality tool of the ancients who would use physical and emotional clues to assess whether you were an earth, water, fire or air person, much like the four main houses in astrology, though the assessment didn't always correspond to your sun sign.

In brief, Earth people are typically practical, grounded, doers; Water people are emotional, feeling empathic types; Fire people are the bold, assertive, intuitive types; Air people are the idealist thinkers.

Often we are an interesting mix of elements with one or two functions more dominant. So if you know you are, for example, a fire type and you find the fire breath compromised then it could mean that your natural energy is low and needs refining through focus on the fire breath.

The breath as healer is an interesting mindfulness practice and by bringing awareness to the whole function of respiration much can be learned about yourself.

Not only can the breath help with pain, and the ensuing psychological blocks we place around 'holding' onto pain, but it is a great alleviator of stress and anxiety.

For instance, if you suffer from panic attacks you will understand how anxiety can often contribute to a nausea in the stomach. This leads to a fear of an attack and so the body starts to prepare for its typical survival mechanism: increased adrenaline and cortisol are typical, and then in rushes the fight, flight or freeze mode. We get sweaty palms, the heart races and this, for the panic attacker, leads to a complete disturbance and often breakdown with the breath.

By gaining control of the breath the panic attack can subside. Often control is gained simply by telling ourselves that our physical symptoms are a normal result of our survival mechanism and that in reality we have nothing to fear.

However, you can also use the grounding effect of earth breath – breathing in and out of the nose only – to bring yourself, out of the overactive, panicking heady space of an attack back into the body. By engaging with the breath in a definite way you are gaining control of your fears and your very physical and sometimes scary response to them.

So for regular panic attackers, or those who are feeling overwrought with stress and anxiety, I recommend you go outside every day and practice the earth breath (in and out through the nose) to ground yourself. Daylight, whether it's sunny or not, helps produce melatonin which works with the brain's natural serotonin levels, an important neurotransmitter for regulating our feel-good moods and beating depression.

You can also combine the earth breath with a concentration of breathing in and out of the feet accompanied by the visualisation of roots coming out of your feet, curling down into the earth where they are firmly anchored. This will all serve to ground you firmly and reduce panic levels.

Whether stressed or not, the breath is undoubtedly a great calmer and mood changer, bringing stability and balance.

As a result, the modern mindfulness movement advocates several breath exercises, especially the brief breath exercise, encouraging practitioners to build in several three-minute breath practices throughout the day.

I have found this practice is be a super pause button in between key moments of the day, particularly when ending one job and moving onto the next. The whole aspect of what I call beginnings and endings will be the feature of the next and final Step but the breath can play an important part of maintaining a mindful day, celebrating mini beginnings and endings from dawn to dusk.

One of my mindfulness clients, a UK investment banker, reported during an 8 week MBCT programme I was running that the three-minutes breathing exercise (BS) had saved him millions of dollars of business.

"I'd finished something online and was about to check out Facebook or another social media account while waiting for a booked conference call with a client in New York when I heard Laura's voice saying now's a good time to do a three-minute BS," he said.

"Thank God, I did the breathing exercise. I was so focused in my mind and present in my body that I was able to tackle successfully what turned out to be an acrimonious call from this client and save millions of dollars of business. I know if I'd been playing online instead I'd have probably lost the client by not being alert, or found myself in difficulties."

As this client demonstrates being mindful can operate throughout your day and these simple techniques, when incorporated at a core level, can be life-changing.

So for the three-minute breathing space, sit in your chair with both your feet flat on the floor, or stand, and bring the focus of your awareness to your immediate state. For the first minute scan your presence, tuning at the start into your body and physical sensations, then your emotions and finally your thoughts. As you tune in observe yourself but without comment, criticism or judgement. Free the mind from some running commentary on your present state. Just note and move on.

The next minute you narrow the focus of your awareness to the breath, simply watching it coming in and out of the body, if the mind wanders, which it will do (that's minds for you), simply bring your attention back to the breath.

The final minute is spent widening the focus of awareness again to your current state, so tuning back into body here in the room or wherever it is. You can now use the breath to explore with gentle curiosity any tightness, or holding or pain in the body, but again without commentary or criticism. Just with the spotlight of the impartial observer.

Then afterwards coming back into the 'world' and noting how your mood has altered.

As stated, the three-minute breathing space is simple yet, as with all breath practices, subtly powerful. It can be morphed into longer or shorter moments, speckled throughout the day that help you retune into a mindful state and enable you to reconnect with some of the other steps we've covered so far.

It also helps us reconnect with a deeper rhythm of existence, the inhale and exhale of life around us that gently holds the rocking movement, a continuous beat of all living forms that drums on automatically in the background of our lives.

Knowing your breath is an important facet of knowing yourself. If nothing else, at least once a day spend some time with your breath.

Watch it, be with it, get up close and personal with it – it's what keeps you alive.

STEP NINE
BEGINNINGS & ENDINGS

Time past and time future
What might have been and what has been
Point to one end, which is always present.

Burnt Norton, T. S. Eliot.

So here we are almost done. You will hopefully now read to the end of these final pages and close this book...and then you will begin something else.

If you like reading no doubt you are planning your next book. See, the next beginning is already being lined up.

And that is the pattern of life.

Arguably, life is a series of beginnings and endings. Within our daily existence these are often negligible, imperceptible. We finish one little task, ready to start the next: eat breakfast, tidy up crockery, buy a ticket, get on the train.

Many of these beginnings and endings are routines we know well, creating the backdrop of our lives. However, they quickly morph into autopilot mode which we discussed earlier and take us away from being more mindful about the minutiae which make up our lives.

Then there are the bigger, more obvious beginnings and endings: leaving school but going to university, leaving home but finding a new place, changing jobs and embarking on a new one.

Or the ultimate: having a child, burying a parent.

We rarely connect fully with life, especially its little events. We congratulate ourselves on the big moments with certain celebration rituals that mark the significance of the closing of some important moment or the starting of something new, such as birthdays, a new home, a new job, a new year.

However, we forget that life is a series of beginnings and endings as we rush through it, from moment to moment. We think we can multi-task without pause or reflection. Yet, as we considered earlier, the modern day mindfulness movement and MRI brain scan research out of Harvard are proving that this is not the case.

The simple practice of the one to three minute breathing exercises, or what I call 'arrival', enables us to acknowledge the constant stream of endings and beginnings by punctuating them with a structured breathing pause. As a result, instead of the daily lurch from moment to moment, we are regularly learning to savour the present.

So, as we discussed in the last Step, Know Your Breath, if you are about to do something new, take some time to settle, wherever you are, and arrive.

Let's take a meeting for example. Make sure you get there with a few moments to spare so that you 'arrive' properly. Settle in your chair. Get out everything you need and then literally press the 'pause' button. Without speaking or making contact with anyone, take in a few deep breaths, assimilate what's going on around you, and sit up straight, adopting a posture which for you encapsulates the notion of noble grace.

Then tune into the room. Feel the chair beneath your thighs, a sense of yourself here in this space. Tune into your breath, noting where it starts in your body at this moment. And then tune into the energies coming out to play in the room. You don't have to spend long or labour at this. The whole exercise can take just a few moments. To those around you it would appear as though you are composing yourself.

This act of 'coming into the present' is deeply empowering and centring, giving a sense of deeper presence and purpose.

Another exercise, as discussed from the last chapter, Know Your Breath, is the 3 minute Breathing Space, again worth practicing in the gap between completion and commencement of any moment of the day.

This witnessing of our small completions means that we are recognising our triumphs through the day, giving weight and value to the small, making them significant, rather than petty or inconsequential. As a result, we are valuing our daily existence, rather than pushing it away in a desire for the bigger, grander moments that we believe hold greater importance.

As the old adage goes: 'life is what happens while you are busy making other plans'.

By bringing consciousness to the small and everyday we are imbuing meaning to these moments. This, in turn, serves to construct a greater sense of self-worth and confidence, as we start to value what is really happening in our daily existence. Eventually we realise how much we truly live our lives.

Awareness can start with simple tasks at home, as well as at work.

I remember listening on the radio to a vivid testimony of a mother with young children, in her late 30's, who was dying of breast cancer. As she stepped away from the big career in the last year of her life she became bewitched by the beauty of the everyday. She reported how she loved watching and recording the little things her children did or said which she'd previously missed while sat at her desk at work.

She had also found that washing up was an amazing joy rather than a tedium. It meant from the beginning to the end of task that she could watch life magically unfold outside the kitchen window in her garden. It became a spell-binding film, not something to be autopiloted. She was very present and, in that moment, she realised she was seeing for the first time the true splendour of life in the small.

By bringing awareness to the beginning and ending of the small, time, instead of contracting, seems to expand and the days become fuller.

As the Indian poet, Tagore writes: 'A butterfly counts, not in months but in moments, and has time enough.'

Obviously, a deeper consideration of beginnings and endings means that we bring our relationship with time into greater focus. Some jobs can seem interminable and frustration grows if we feel we aren't accomplishing something. We are desperate that these issues or jobs will end and we are relieved when they do.

However, this kind of protracted relationship with time teaches us much. We are able to develop the powerful and important qualities of patience, resilience and acceptance of the difficult.

With clients who struggle to accept they are making progress or are making the changes they desire I often compare this process to long distance walking.

I once walked the St James Camino – the ancient pilgrimage which runs one thousand miles from Le Puy en Velay in France to Santiago de Compostela in Northern Spain – with a group of friends. The journey seemed interminable as we were doing sections each year over a six year period. Some days were joyous, other days the distances seemed cruel and the terrain impossible.

I remember one day very clearly, finally coming to a hilltop peak *en route* to the Pyrenean mountains and our crossing into Spain. We'd been steadily stomping towards this summit for the whole of the morning since our departure after breakfast at some dreadful hour.

The arrival at the end of the climb up this hill felt like a remarkable achievement but, as we gazed into the distance, the rest of the day's walking stretched out before us and seemed daunting. Our spirits sunk a little.

And then I looked back.

Wow. Suddenly I could see way, way in the distance from where I had come, and a deeper sense of accomplishment waved over me.

How often do we do the same in life? We are so busy concentrating on our future horizons that we forget to look back and acknowledge what we have achieved to date, and how far we have come.

How often do we 'arrive'? Actually press the pause button and savour the moment at the end or beginning of each small job, let alone each big job, instead of rushing from task to task, and properly acknowledge our success.

Emeritus Professor Mark Williams, from the Oxford Mindfulness Centre, who has pioneered the introduction of the modern day mindfulness movement in the UK, tells a Buddhist story in his influential book, *Mindfulness: a practical guide to Finding Peace in a Frantic World* (Williams & Penman, 2011), which addresses the same concept. I will retell it here.

'A king wanted to move palace but because he feared that his enemies might take advantage of this to attack him and steal his treasures, he summoned his trusted general. 'My friend,' he said, 'I have to move palace and must do so within twenty-four hours. You have been my trusted servant and soldier for a long time and I do not trust anyone but you to help me. Only you know the network of underground passages beneath the two palaces. If you manage to do this in the twenty-four hour deadline and move all my precious treasures by yourself I will give you and your family your freedom. You can retire and as a reward for your long faithful service I will give you a portion of my wealth and lands so that you can settle, and your children and grandchildren and subsequent generations will be financially secure.'[1]

'The day came when the treasures were to be moved. The general worked hard. He was not young and it was tough. He persisted. He knew that after twenty-four hours it would be unsafe. With minutes to spare he completed the job. He went to his king who was delighted. The king was a man of his word and gave the trusted general the portion of treasure he'd promised and the deeds to some of the most beautiful and fertile lands in the kingdom.

'The general returned home and took a bath. As he lay there he looked back on all he had achieved in his life, and he relaxed. He felt with great satisfaction that he could now retire, that his major tasks were finished. And for that moment he had a sense of completeness. The story ends here.'

As Mark then asks: do you know what that moment is like – a sense that things have been done, properly completed?

Can you make space and time for truly acknowledging where you are on your Camino and celebrate what you've accomplished? Whether it is just during today or over a longer distance?

What I love about this story is that the general takes a bath. This is no flamboyant celebration with champagne and a huge party. His acknowledgement is simple and very personal. It's a private exercise in holding the moment.

Sometimes the big ritualistic celebrations are so overblown and externalised that they enable us to avoid going into the feelings we might be holding about whatever we have achieved.

Without proper connection we can disassociate emotionally because there might be loss, hurt or pain attached that we want to avoid feeling, as well as joy, and so we lose the opportunity to feel, absorb, explore and experience what this ritual truly means for us.

Eventually we get locked in the goldfish bowl moment, the assumed seven second memory span of a goldfish that constantly swims round the bowl thinking its seeing something new and saying: that looks nice, that looks nice.

When we are in goldfish bowl mood everything becomes superficial and significance is lost because we don't give ourselves time to explore what beginnings and endings mean for us. We are choosing denial rather than a deeper connection with our true feelings.

Instead, during these big moments, we need to carve out some time for ourselves whereby we register and properly connect with the moment.

What do beginnings and endings mean for you? Think of large significant ones to date. How did you deal with them? How did you celebrate? What emotions are there in the background when you recall those times? Are you denying feeling those emotions?

Then look at your life today and see which moments stand out and why? What did you learn at the beginning and ending of those times? How have they contributed to who you are today? What qualities did they give you?

If you have a big beginning and ending looming on the horizon how are you now planning on recognising this important milestone?

I once lived in a beautiful house, perched high in the mountains, overlooking a valley far below and the mountain peaks in front. I loved this home. I had helped plan and build it. Much of 'me' had gone into this creative process. It was a magical place and I felt blessed to live there. Sadly, due to painful family circumstances, the day came when this loved home had to be sold.

On the very last morning I decided that I would sit truly present with the experience of saying my goodbye.

As I sat on a chair on the balcony in the wintry sun I tuned into all my senses. I listened to the sounds around me; I felt the sensations on my skin and body; I tasted the snow and the air on my tongue; I looked carefully at the scene both far away, mid-range and close to, even studying the grain on the wood cladding on the house wall.

I tuned into the deep well of sadness but also recalled the joys of being there over the years.

As a ritual I made an icy heart out of snow and watched it slowly melt in the sun.

And then I got in my car and drove away.

I have not been back since. A new beginning was started.

And yet, even now, I can bring that moment immediately up to the forefront of my mind and be whisked right back. Suddenly the moment is not lost. That home is not lost and I am there again. My experience is still richly with me. The moment was truly honoured and preserved and, in some way, I have transcended time by sealing that final morning for all of time in my mind.

As the quote at the start of the chapter from T S Eliot's Burnt Norton states:

> Time past and time future
> What might have been and what has been
> Point to one end, which is always present.

This kind of self-observation, along with self-reflection, are important aspects of the mindfulness process. They enable us to learn and grow.

Mindfulness helps us become more aware of our behaviours, many of which are unconscious reactions that have been honed over the years. In this awareness comes freedom because instead of reacting blindly we can, instead, *choose* how we want to respond.

That is empowerment. That is the joy and strength of mindfulness in our lives.

Many spiritual practices use the end of the day as a moment of self-reflection. At bedtime the quest is to reflect on the day and observe yourself interacting with those around you, looking at what you can learn, especially in terms of self-improvement and what you can discard. The key is not to dwell on issues and self-flagellate but to observe, note and then let go.

Try tuning into your day while in bed before turning out the light, reading a book or whatever ritual you employ to prepare for the end of being awake and to call in the beginning of sleep. Watch yourself, like a film, during the day from when you awoke through to this moment. Note your interactions with those in your life that day; how you felt, thought, sensed and what you did.

Accept what you said, and what was not said, whether what you felt was 'right or wrong', or 'good or bad'. Then, without commentary or

criticism, especially of others, let it all go, knowing that the next day is a
blank sheet on which you can write again.

In this exercise I must stress it is important not to get bogged
down in one's thoughts, obsessions and reactions when recapping the day
but to detach. With practice one observes blockages and regular
obsessive or compulsive thoughts and can learn more about one's
behaviour in the process.

This healing practice over time brings a greater recognition of the
power of acceptance as a route to forgiveness, both of self and of others

We instinctively do the same exercise at the end of each year with
the habit of looking back over the past year and contemplation of the next
with a host of New Year's resolutions lined up.

Arguably, of course, the New Year is just another day but a ritual
has developed around the beginning and endings of the year whereby we
reflect on our 'old' life and decide a different course of action for the new.
Whether we keep the promises to ourselves or not, the New Year has
often been the kick-start to the abandonment of many a habit from
quitting smoking to changing life-style and diet.

In the end it's a celebration of the dying year and of what's to
come. It's about recognising and appreciating potentiality in change and
transformation.

So at the end of a retreat sitting under that lime tree what did I
find? At the end of the silence and beginning of coming back to life I spoke
to the woman whom I felt I'd insulted to tell her of how I found her like
the beautiful tree, rooted and very present instead of stubborn, strong
but also flexible. I wanted to start again with her.

As I came back to life this time I also found that I wanted to share
what I'd discovered and decided to start my new beginning by writing this
book.

For those of you interested in taking a deliberate step out of life
then retreats of any kind are a superb structure for creating the right
environment. Different spiritual and religious organisations offer a range
of opportunities that a simple search online will unearth. They can
incorporate silence or guided meditation practices, either as an individual
or in a group. The retreat journey should be about helping you detach
from life and then bring you back with whatever insights you have gained.

And now we are nearing the end of this book.

As I look out of my study window it is early Spring after a weird non-Winter. Catkins are already glowing fluorescent yellow on the tree next door. Bluetits are dancing in and out of the bare branches on bushes and shrubs still to flower, and a fat pigeon is spinning round on my washing line.

My naughty resident fox is slinking behind the back of shed. I can see the mail van going by in the road beyond. The desk clock counts on and, in the background, I hear my washing machine whirring. I can smell the heady hyacinth bowl and the pungent left-overs of my teacup. I can still taste the tea's sweetness on the tip of my tongue and the insides of my cheeks.

I feel a weird mixture of sadness that this book is nearly complete and elation that soon I will get to share my work. And I know that having spent a small moment honouring the completion of this achievement I will remember this moment for the rest of my life with a sense of awe, respect and gratitude.

So I ask you to tune into what you are feeling right now at the end. Perhaps complete a similar exercise as above, running through your senses, emotions, thoughts and impulses so you remember how you felt on completing this book.

My final impulse now is to punch the air and shout out an affirming 'YES!!'

What have you learned and how do you plan to go forward? What is your next beginning out of this ending?

If nothing else, remember that life is here to be enjoyed. So get on with it but don't dash through it – take time to savour and celebrate mindfully each precious, precious amazing moment.

I now proudly write: THE END.

POST SCRIPT - STEP TEN
AND NOW MEDITATE

Many people asked me while writing this how I could talk about mindfulness without mentioning meditation. The aim of this book is to demonstrate that you don't have to sit Zen-like or Ohm on a mat with dozens of people to lead a mindful life. You can just get on with it.

Mindfulness is about knowing yourself. It is the power of conscious self-awareness that enables change and transformation through self-knowledge. In that by knowing yourself and your behaviours, instead of knee-jerk reactions to life you can take a step back at any given moment and ask yourself how to do I want to respond. That is choice. That is expression of free will. That is empowerment.

However, like all mindfulness proponents, I would urge that meditation is the powerhouse for maintaining this practice of self-awareness.

So a sneaky Step Ten would be 'And Now Meditate'.

If you have started to practice aspects of the nine steps to a mindful life you are probably already noticing the effects of taking a daily time-out so that the next and final step ten, to sit with a deeper awareness, will come naturally.

Again, an online search will bring up many theories, techniques and meditation schools. Meditating regularly in a group is rewarding and a very rich experience, and you will find in your local area many different approaches.

However, a daily individual practice, whether just for a few minutes or longer, is the bedrock of the mindful self.

Here are a few guidelines:

Sit on a chair, or the floor, or even lie on the floor if that is preferable, but not lying on a bed, and make contact with the ground. Make sure that your legs are uncrossed and your feet are flat on the ground. Allow your hands to settle in your lap, not clenched or clasped, possibly with one on top of the other (different spiritual schools have different thoughts about this aspect but don't get hung up about this at the start).

Then gently close your eyes, or, if this feels uncomfortable, lower the eyelids and direct your gaze gently to a spot on the floor just in front of you.

Now make contact with your face, in particular tune into your eyes; are they straining to see some imaginary screen of thoughts and images? Allow the eyes to soften. I often bring my awareness to my cheekbones to do this.

Then tune into your jawline, top and bottom; again we often clench our teeth, so soften here. It helps to drop the tongue into the well behind the bottom teeth; it is often fixed to the roof of our mouth as a constant prelude to speaking and so makes it an overused organ.

Now become aware of your posture. The spine should be straight and ideally you should be sitting away from the back of the chair so that you are self-supporting. I like the phrase 'to sit with noble grace' as my little mantra for getting into this pose. There is something beautifully ennobling about sitting in meditation.

Next bring your focus to your presence here on the floor or the chair and tune in to your body as you do with the three minute breathing space, bringing awareness to where your body makes contact with the chair or ground, noting sensations, emotions, thoughts and impulses and then letting them go. Just observing without commentary, criticism or judgement.

Now it's time, as with the three minute breathing space, to make contact with your breath. Note where it comes into the body at this time and just follow it in and out, getting up close to the breath. Feel it coming in cold and going out warm. Even say to yourself, if you want: 'I am breathing in, I am breathing out'. And simply sit here with the breath.

The mind will wander, it's what minds do. You simply congratulate yourself that you have noticed you've drifted off and come back to the breath.

Many meditators like to see the distracting thoughts as waves on the ocean: you are the ocean not the wave, or clouds scudding in the sky: you are the sky not the clouds. We are not our thoughts. They come and go and like clouds or waves. We can watch them pass and return simply to following our breath... until you stop.

And that is meditating. Sounds easy but is a discipline often hard to maintain as life wants to crowd in and steal you away. Regular meditators chose a regular time every day to sit in meditative stillness in a bid to carve out this valuable moment, come what may.

Many set timed interval bells on a phone or tablet to signal stage posts or endings. There are also many apps that have grown up around the mindfulness movement such as Headspace that offer this kind of support function.

Explore. Remember that curiosity is a vital mindfulness attribute. Explore your wonderful vibrant life with joy and love coming back each day to repose, to sit in meditation as a download and recharge ready for the next day, whatever it might bring.

Then a cloud passed, and the pool was empty.
Burnt Norton – T.S Eliot. (T.S.Eliot, 2001)

MINDFULNESS BACKGROUND

In the main, three schools dominate the modern day mindfulness movement which has emerged out of the meeting of late 20th and early 21st century cognitive behavioural psychology theories with some ancient Zen and Tibetan Buddhist practices.

MINDFULNESS BASED STRESS REDUCTION (MBSR)

This is probably the first main school of thought, predominantly US led, following the modern father of the mindfulness movement, Jon Kabat-Zinn. His main works are listed in the Bibliography Section.

Kabat-Zinn, a psychologist at the University of Massachusetts, became involved with meditation through yoga and realised the immense personal benefits he was experiencing.

He wondered what it would be like to introduce some of these techniques to those he was treating at a clinic for chronic pain sufferers. The results were startlingly positive and became the foundation of today's movement.

Kabat-Zinn has pioneered the development of MBSR internationally. His techniques are being adopted by many leading global companies and organisations, particularly in the US, such as Google, AOL and General Foods. Their case studies can be read on online.

He has also run mindful workshops at Davos, the annual meeting in Switzerland of the world's leaders, introducing those in power to the power of meditation and mindfulness.

MINDFULNESS BASED COGNITIVE THERAPY (MBCT)

UK follower of Kabat-Zinn, Emeritus Professor Mark Williams, is the main proponent of MBCT style mindfulness in the UK. Having established the highly successful Oxford Centre for Mindfulness at Oxford University his eight-week MBCT programme at the Centre is continually oversubscribed and is being introduced in classes around the country, as well as in hospitals, mental health programmes, businesses and schools.

MBCT is very similar to MBSR but has a depression component which has brought it to the attention of the UK's health regulator, National Institute for Health and Care Excellence, (NICE), which now recommends the 8 week MBCT programme as part of a care package for those with depression, stress and anxiety.

Professor William's seminal work with co-writer, Danny Penman: *Mindfulness: A Practical Guide to Finding Peace in a Frantic World* is consistently in the top ten of non-fiction paperbacks and is an excellent

ACCEPTANCE AND COMMITMENT THEORY (ACT)

ACT is a clinical behaviour theory which combines the power of self-observation with acceptance and mindfulness strategies to change one's approach to life. It is seen as developing 'psychological flexibility'.

Very much in line with the approach in this book, Nine Steps to a Mindful Life (without meditating), ACT psychologists and users of mindfulness don't believe that one has to meditate to live mindfully; that simple skills can bring about personal transformation.

ACT considers three main areas –Diffusion – distancing and separation from painful or difficult thoughts, emotions and memories; Acceptance – allowing painful and difficult thoughts, emotions and beliefs to surface so that they can be accepted – come and go without a struggle; Contact – coming very much into the immediate present moment with curiosity and openness.

ELLEN LANGER

Known as the 'Mother of Mindfulness', Langer was the first female professor of psychology to be appointed at Harvard University and for forty years has pioneered research into mindfulness, initially outside of the work of proponents such as Kabat-Zinn.

Running her own 'Mindfulness Lab' at Harvard the core of her work encompasses the three concepts of uncertainty, conditionality and possibility. As she states, she has discovered that an important truth about human psychology is that certainty is a cruel mind-set, hardening our minds against possibility and closing us to the world we live in.

She believes that mindfulness is the simple act of 'noticing things' and that a mindful approach to any activity involves the continuous creation of new categories, openness to new information and an implicit awareness of more than one perspective.

She also believes that you can develop a sense of mindfulness without meditation.

MINDFULNESS EXERCISES

STEP ONE – TREAT EACH DAY AS IF IT'S YOUR LAST

Head Voices
See if you can name some: planner, problem solver, organiser, pacifier, boss, fantasiser, daydreamer, critic, judge of both self and others.

When Time Stood Still
Close your eyes, settle into your chair, place your feet flat on the floor and just listen and connect to your breathing for three breaths. Then say to yourself: 'When time stood still I...' Where were you? Who were you with? What did you think and feel, and what sensations were in your body or are now rising as you do the exercise? Sit with whatever arises and then analyse what happens to you under the categories: Body Sensations, Emotions, Thoughts and Actions.

Death Denial Package
Can you identify what's yours?

If This Is My Last Day – What Are My Values?
Right now check-in and ask yourself what are you doing in this moment? Wherever you are reading this, breathe deeply three times and just sense the chair or bed or ground which is supporting you, and connect with it. Then take the moment to reconnect with your body sensations, emotions, thoughts and desires to act. Tune in and ask yourself if this is my last day what would I take away with me from this moment? Savour the experience fully, watching what happens to you. There's no need to rush, let time look after itself. Allow life to meet you, absorb you, become you.

And then ask yourself, 'What do I value most?' Perhaps find three things you value; you might find more but don't strain to make a list or you will slip into the active 'doing' mode, just note what instantly comes to mind.

You can try writing a letter to loved ones. Ask why you love them, what makes you happy that you are in each other's lives and why you would miss them. See if you can sense the qualities that they hold and also any message that you would want to give them.

Perhaps plan to tune in three times each day to your experience, setting an alarm on your phone, to ask yourself, 'if this is my last day what would I take away from this experience?'

And if you are 'treating each day as if it's your last' what would you do differently today, what would need to change or be incorporated in some way?

STEP TWO - GO SLOWER

Task Isolation
Have a go at seeing if you can isolate your tasks even while reading this or during the next fifteen to thirty minutes. Perhaps say, 'I'm reading, I am drinking coffee, I am scratching my head, I am looking out of the window, I am watching the wind in the leaves, I am looking at my smart phone, I am checking the time...

Multi-Tasking Review
During the day see if you can spot your attempts at 'multi-tasking' and check yourself. Decide which is more important and just do that task mindfully with focus. As you slow down you will find greater clarity and, ironically, greater efficiency as you do each task with full attention.

What's It Like to Stop?
What would it be like to stop, right now? Stop and reflect on how you can make your life slower? What would you need to jettison? What do you need to do less of, more of? Close your eyes and perhaps remember what you had found when you did the 'When Time Stood Still' exercise?

Values
Also tune back into your values that you considered in Step One. Aligning ourselves with our values helps us to lead a more meaningful life but also helps us become less task-orientated. We step away from rushing around to achieve our goals and discover a slower tempo.

Chicken Little Thinking – One Job At A Time

So what kind of Chicken Little thinking do you tell yourself? Would the sky really fall in if you didn't get a certain something done today? Do you have lists to get you through the day? Can they be streamlined? Are you over-committing?

In the main, we need to prioritise better to give ourselves more time. Would you be more efficient if you just did one certain kind of task, such as organising your expenses, on one day each week or month rather than doing it in dribs and drabs between larger jobs?

As considered in Step One, practise doing one job to the very end without interruption before starting another. Try right now while you are reading this. Give yourself permission to read to the end of this chapter so a section is completed before you pick up your phone, tablet, pen, or whatever.

STEP THREE – AUTOPILOT: WHO'S DRIVING THE CAR?

Stepping Out of Autopilot - Food

So choose an item of food; it doesn't have to be a raisin. It can be fruit, cheese, bread, whatever. And from the moment of choice study yourself. Forget that childhood admonishment 'don't play with your food' and play with it!

Look at the food carefully. See it for the very first time like an alien would arriving from out of space. What does it feel like in your hands? What does it smell like? If you squidged it by your ears what can you hear? Take your time with all these sensory moments. Savour them and watch at each stage your bodily reactions, your emotions, thoughts and impulses (what you feel the urge to do).

Then when you have finished the observation period place the food to your lips and note what happens to your body, emotions, thoughts and actions. See if you can identify when the process of digestion takes places and what physical sensations that involves for you. Finally place whatever food you have chosen in your mouth and, without chewing, note again the physical, emotional and mental processes that are happening. Then slowly chew, noting everything again before the final act of swallowing.

Stepping Out of Autopilot - Routines

Consider some of your daily routines and try to bring full awareness to the activity. Try brushing your teeth with the other hand. Play with mindful dressing, showering, preparing meals. Take the whole activity apart and watch exactly what happens moment by moment, again, making contact with your bodily sensations, emotions, thoughts and impulses. The whole process becomes a waking meditation.

Stepping Out of Autopilot - Driving

And if you really want to tackle the autopilot literally, try mindful driving – but with care. Traffic police are taught to talk through every action when driving in active situations so it can all be officially recorded. Try doing the same in your own head or out loud: "turning key clockwise in the lock with the right hand, checking the mirror…." and then when in traffic talk through the driving experience, such as, "pulling up to red traffic light, four cars away from the junction, light changing to green, going into first gear…"

Stepping Out of Autopilot – Mobile Phones & Tablets

Just become aware of your phone and tablet. Where are they now while you are reading this? How often have you stopped to check them, possibly without realising? Continuing during the rest of day and week just become aware of how often your devices pull for your attention. What would it be like to switch them off for an hour…or longer, giving yourself a break from their obsessive draw?

And if you can't switch it off ask yourself what is getting in the way? What is the fear that prevents you from being out of touch, even momentarily? What is the brain-chatter that robs you of a rare moment of complete connection with the reality of life at this very moment and this very time?

STEP FOUR - HAVING A MEANINGFUL RELATIONSHIP WITH YOURSELF

Tune Into Yourself

So take time, why not here, right now and give yourself a breather? Just take one small moment for you, wherever you are reading this. Perhaps you are at home, on a train, outside. Just put the book or reading device down and sit, or, if circumstances dictate, stand.

Tune in firstly to what's happening around you. Witness yourself as though in suspended animation in a moving film. Then tune in at a deeper sensory level. If outside, feel the wind or sun on your skin, or if inside, the warmth or coolness of the air around you.

Tune into the noises of your immediate environment. Don't try to force them away. Absorb them. Become part of the sound flow. Then visually connect with something that catches your eye. Explore it momentarily as you did with the raisin or chosen food in the autopilot exercise.

Can you smell anything? What olfactory (smell) sensations are present? If you are on the way to work, then perhaps someone's coffee cup or yours is catching your powerful smell receptors.

Now just watch all of your thoughts, emotions, body sensations, impulses. Just be with them, accepting without judgment or criticism. If the mind wanders and starts wanting to scratch at some niggling issue, tagging in your usual favourite commentary, note the issue and park it. It's not part of this exercise.

Congratulate yourself that you have noticed the mind is off doing its 'thing' and just come back to sitting or standing with a sense of yourself, reminding yourself that this is about stopping just for a few moments in silence, in reverie.

Over time you will become aware of regular thought patterns or body behaviours in different circumstances. Perhaps you find there is always one special time of the day that you enjoy this exercise? Ask yourself what that's about? What makes this a special time? Why do you give yourself permission to 'stop' at this time of day? Why not at other times? What would it be like to change the time of your practice?

Reconnect With Your Values
Perhaps in these moments you can take time to remind yourself of your three chosen values, that we considered in Step One, bringing them deeper into the fibre of your being and giving yourself permission to make them an active part of your life. Are you living your values right now? What needs to happen to bring them in?

Who Am I?

Another exercise in reverie is the self-affirmation exercise called 'Who am I?' It can start with something simple such as: 'I am a man'. 'I am a woman'. Then build. 'I am a mother', 'I am a father', 'I am a daughter, a son'. 'I am an aunty, uncle.' 'I am English, American.' 'I am a teacher'. 'I am a dog-owner.' 'I am a house-owner'. 'I am loved.' 'I am lover'.

Always start with the expression; 'I am...' and allow the list to expand and flow, again without judgement or criticism. Just simply be with the many faces, statuses and essences that construct you. Note how they can change over the days, weeks, months. Ask yourself what these changes might mean for you but without any great attachment to their outcome.

If a change in 'face' or status disturbs or causes a rise in emotion just note its strong reactions but remember how many others 'faces' are still an active part of your daily life, sustaining and holding you. For instance, I find it tough to say 'I'm a daughter' since the death of my parents. I often feel sad about that but I'm strengthened by the other 'faces' I daily inhabit.

My Qualities

Another practice is to identify which qualities are currently operating in your life. Perhaps kick off with assessing what qualities seem innate in your being and are readily part of your essential self. You can add them to the Who Am I list. 'I am confident, I am caring, I am determined...'

Then look at the qualities that are becoming more active in your life right now. What qualities are the current conditions of your life demanding you to discover? Are you being asked to become more resilient, patient, forgiving?

And looking forward, what qualities are still needing to be unearthed, that you aren't expressing in your life at this time?

STEP FIVE - HAVING A MEANINGFUL RELATIONSHIP WITH OTHERS

Connect Right Now With Lost Ones!

How many of your relationships have drifted into ether world? Is there anyone who you feel you should call right now? Why not pick up the phone and tune into their voice again. Or go one better: arrange to meet.

Stranger Eyes

Try this today: make a different connection with whomever you meet regularly during your daily routine and who is not part of your immediate circle at home or work. Perhaps it's the barrista at your favourite coffee shop, the official in the ticket office at your train station, someone crammed into the same tube carriage as you. Instead of ordering that coffee and going through your perfunctory routine around the purchase, make a full connection with the server. Smile, look in their eyes in friendship and wait for their eyes to make a connection back.

And then tune into the energy change. How do you feel? Has something changed? Note the subtle body signals that you can now pick up. How has the Other now chosen to respond to you? For those in service jobs it can be a faceless experience as the public comes and goes, and never 'sees' you. The person who finally 'sees' you makes all the difference. You look forward to seeing and serving them again.

Connect Right Now At work

What would it be like to take that experience into the workplace? Try talking to people's eyes, using your eyes to make a real connection. You'll soon find how this is a different relationship from a 'head' connection. It's more heart centred.

Instead of emailing a colleague who's in the same office as you, walk over to their desk occasionally and make contact. What do you know about their personal lives? What would it be like to learn that the mousey woman in IT is 'into' flamenco dancing? How does that change your perception of her?

Would you now start to see her as someone more 'real', more substantial, than simply the mousey woman in IT? As we found in the previous chapter's 'I am' exercise we all inhabit more than one face.

The Car & Train Test

Next time you are driving and stuck in a line of traffic, with vehicles trying to join the queue from side roads, note what happens when you let someone in to the line in a friendly manner. Usually other drivers will follow suit. If you do it begrudgingly, or not at all, then the atmosphere around you is not so 'giving' and those around you are less likely to offer up a space. Offer your seat on a train to someone less fortunate than yourself and see how that impacts on others around you.

Mood Contagion - Reading The Room At Work
First, using techniques we discussed in Step four, scan yourself and tune into your immediate emotional experience so you have identified your own current emotional state before arriving into the work or group space. Then when you enter see if you can 'read' the room and sense what is happening there.

Can you tune in and name an emotion that is sitting in the environment. Does it feel happy, sad, angry? More importantly what happens to you? As you attune can you feel yourself absorbing and adopting to the herd mood?

What would it be like to reject the mood if it's uncomfortable and negative, and mindfully adopt your own more positive mindset? Perhaps sit at your desk, or wherever is suitable, and by taking time to be with yourself, as in the last chapter, try emanating something different. What happens to the herd mentality now? Does your positive vibe begin to affect those around you?

Mood Contagion - Reading The Room At Home
Next try this at home, or whenever you are, with your closest companions. Read the group vibe. What is really happening? When you, as a family, or as friends, are sitting watching TV or eating dinner together what is being communicated by the group?

What happens if you project another emotion what impact does that have on the group?

Again take it into your closest of relationships. If you sit in silence together what is really being transmitted between you? And how does this make you react? What is it like to look deeply into your loved ones' eyes on a more regular basis?

What's Your Anger About?
Next time you are feeling angry ask yourself if you are scared about not being seen or heard in a given situation.

STEP SIX - TOO MANY WASTED WORDS
Music & Feelings

Recall a piece of music that makes you feel sad with memories attached, or another that brings joy to your heart. Perhaps play the pieces now and note which part of your body responds to the sounds and sit with the emotions that lie there. Feel the resonance inside of you. When the music is finished sit in the silence and note how the soundwaves continue their work in and around you. What part of you is the 'unplucked heart' that is resonating? Is there a part of your body that is responding to the after-sounds? What is it feeling? If it had a voice what would it be saying to you?

Watch Your Chatter

Watch your daily discourse with those around you at home, out in the world and at work. Note how often you use the same phrases and how much of conversation is routine. Do you like what you say? Do these phrases serve a real function?

What Happens When You Shop

Watch your own behaviour during your next shopping exchange at the till, wherever you live in the world, and see if you can identify the codes that sit behind this contractual moment.

Workplace Lingo

Think about the language of your working group. Listen to the words that might not have real meaning or a very different meaning in the everyday speak of the wider world you live in.

The next part of the exercise is to assess how much of your daily discourse involves dead words, namely words that have no meaning. How many of these words are so meaningless that they are not understood by much of the herd but are simply repeated so the member can appear to belong?

Home Chatter & The Wider Field

Note what language is typically used in your home for everyday interactions. How do you feel about these phrases? How do they make you react? How do they serve your family group? When is language fun and why? When does it become more formal? What words does your family usually choose for banter and what words for conflict and its resolution? Does one person speak more often than others? Is there someone who rarely has a 'voice' in family matters? What would it be like to include them?

This can, of course, apply across your community spectrum of groups. By listening you will learn much more about the linguistic ebb and flow of your group.

Buttoning It!
Try holding back when in a group or one to one. Let people talk and resist any desire to comment or offer opinion. What happens when you're silent? How does the family, or group, dynamic change? Would your opinion have served any function? Do other people's opinions contribute anything significant, or a deeper meaning?

Swearing - What the *??!?*?
How many swear words are you wasting? Check how many times you swear. Tune into the occasions for swearing? How often is it an expression of anger, or something else? Do you like the sound of these words? Are they necessary? Has swearing become excessive? Try one day or longer without swearing? Note the control this can also give you over other aspects of your daily discourse.

STEP SEVEN - DO SOMETHING DIFFERENT EVERYDAY

Routine Busters
Try brushing your teeth with the other hand, always fun and also a popular anti-autopilot exercise.

Have something different for breakfast, lunch, dinner every day, especially if you're someone who gets stuck in a routine with food. Buy your coffee or groceries from another store. Come home a different way. Watch a different TV programme.

Try switching off your mobile or tablet for an hour, several hours, the whole day. How does that make a difference? What do you find in the silence? Can you cope with not being connected but in the 'unknown'?

Changing Your Life

So, look at your week, your month and think about what you can change. Think of this as fun, as a creative way of living your life. Think of this as play, as waking yourself up, rather than just visiting this world!
If you are a manager study how you are managing change for your team? How do you introduce change? How do you bring creativity and difference into the workplace? Do you encourage staff to change and adopt new practices, or to learn new skills?

What's on your 'bucket list'? What can you start today - a new sport, hobby, language?

Do Technology

Whether you work or not, how often do you resist getting to grips with the latest technological developments for fear of getting it wrong or are scared of facing the frustration technology know-how can encompass? The computer-digital world is constantly upgrading and it's easy to get left behind. So what new function or package could you be learning or downloading now?

STEP EIGHT - KNOW YOUR BREATH

Starting A Relationship With Your Breath

First of all just check right now where your breath is 'entering' the body. Sit or stand, and find out where the journey starts: is it at the nose, the mouth, in the throat, chest or starting deeper down in the abdomen?

Just 'follow' the breath in and out. See if you can stay with the breath. A good way to do this is feel it coming in the nostrils cold and out warm. Are you breathing shortly in the throat area or more deeply from the lower abdomen?

As you sit with the breath what happens? Does it slow down or speed up when you bring your attention to the process? Can you start to play with your breath?

See if you can keep it at the nose for several breaths, and then start taking it down on a journey – breathing in at all the regions mentioned: nostrils, throat, chest, deep abdomen.

Is any region harder than another to breathe from? Perhaps explore that by breathing into the 'tightness' and note what emotions, thoughts, ideas and sensations surface.

Breath Diary & Exercise

Start a breath diary so you can compare how your breath changes over the course of your typical day. It's easier if you set your alarm at certain times of the day for a planned breath check-in. How and where is your breath at breakfast, lunch, dinner, for instance? How is it when you walk into work and then when you leave?

If you use one of the body monitoring devices you can then compare these notes with the daily read-outs to provide extra valuable information about your physical make-up.

How is your breath when you exercise? Are there times when it is higher in the throat or sometimes when you start exercise do you note it's calmer and lower down, meaning that your ability to exercise is greater than when the breath is in 'urgent' mode?

Grounding Breath

Sit on the floor or in a chair, with both feet flat on the floor to 'ground' you. This is important. If you are sitting in a chair spend some time allowing your breath to settle by feeling the chair around you, conscious of it supporting your legs, bum, back, arms. If you are on the floor be aware of the ground supporting your weight. Then breathe in and out three times. If you like, 'in' through the nose and sighing out through the mouth. The outward sighing breath is a great way of releasing stress and physical tension.

Now imagine you have roots extending from your feet deep down into the earth. Allow them to anchor in to the life force energy of this planet before then breathing it up your roots, through all your chakras, pausing at each one to allow its colour to be charged by the energy. If you like you can see each chakra as a ball of colour that is set into spin motion by the earth's rising energy.

So base – red, sacral – orange, solar plexus – yellow, heart – green, throat – blue, third eye – indigo blue, crown – purple.
Then as the energy passes through the crown chakra see it become a white light made up of all colours that then flows down into the aura of

light that surrounds your own body like a protective cloak. Visualise this powerful white light energy as repairing and strengthening your cloak, as it washes away any negativity back into the ground where it is restored into the positive life force.

Elemental Breath

So the earth breath is simply breathing in and out of the nose. As you start the process flex your hands at the wrist as though you are drawing up the earth's energy through your palms. Imagine you are contacting the earth and its strong magnetic force in your mind's eye. Feel it strongly beneath your feet and simply breathe it in.

You can do this for as little as five breaths or longer, depending on your inclination and available time.

The next breath is the water breath. For this you are tuning into water as the all-powerful element that is fundamental to life. We are predominantly water - it makes up to 75% of adult body weight, with 70% of our brains being composed of water and 90% of our lungs. More than 70% of the world is covered in water. So our connection with water is essential.

The water breath involves breathing in through the nose and out of the mouth. As you breath in through the nose visualise you are wading in a beautiful clear stream to a waterfall; as you breath out of your mouth imagine the waterfall cascading gently over your body, its flow caressing your skin and bringing you back in harmony with this vital element.

Again you can do this for as little as five breaths or longer, depending on your inclination and available time.

The fire breath is centred in your heart and is the breath of the assertive force associated with fire that can power through anything. For this breath you breathe in through the mouth and out of the nose. As you breathe in imagine a fire whose coals start to glow with the passing air; as you breathe out put your hand to your heart and visualise the flames from the coals begin to dance. You can then visualise the fire energy of your heart pouring out of all of your sides to the universe.

If you have a cold or chest problems this can be a very healing breath. If you lack energy, or need to find more empowerment for the day, this is also a good engine 'stoker'.

Again do this for as little as five breaths or longer, depending on your inclination and available time.

The air breath is breathing in and out of the mouth. As you know we need air, i.e oxygen, to survive. Like water it is fundamental to life. A good visualisation for this element is to imagine when breathing in through the mouth that there is a pile of leaves above your head, as though these leaves are all the thoughts and ideas that are cluttering your mind. Then with the out breath imagine these thought-leaves are being blown by the wind to the four corners of the world, freeing up your mental space.

Again do this for as little as five breaths or longer, depending on your inclination and available time.

Panic Attacks

For regular panic attackers, or those who are feeling overwrought with stress and anxiety, I recommend you go outside every day and practice the earth breath (in and out through the nose) to ground yourself. Daylight, whether it's sunny or not, helps produce melatonin which works with the brain's natural serotonin levels, an important neurotransmitter for regulating our feel-good moods and beating depression.

You can also combine the earth breath with a concentration of breathing in and out of the feet accompanied by the visualisation of roots coming out at your feet, curling down into the earth where they are firmly anchored. This will all serve to ground you firmly and reduce panic levels.

Three Minute Breathing Space

For the three minute Breathing Space, sit in your chair with both your feet flat on the floor or stand and bring the focus of your awareness to your immediate state. For the first minute scan your presence, tuning at the start into your body and physical sensations, then your emotions and finally your thoughts. As you tune in observe yourself but without comment, criticism or judgement. Free the mind from some running commentary on your present state. Just note and move on.

The next minute you narrow the focus of your awareness to the breath, simply watching it coming in and out of the body, If the mind wanders, which it will do (that's minds for you), simply bring your attention back to the breath.

The final minute is spent widening the focus of awareness again to your current state, so tuning back into body here in the room or wherever it is. You can now use the breath to explore with gentle curiosity any tightness or holding, or pain in the body, but again without commentary or criticism. Just with the spotlight of the impartial observer.

Then afterwards coming back into the 'world' note how your mood has altered.

STEP NINE - BEGINNINGS & ENDINGS

Arrival
Let's take a meeting. Make sure you get there with a few moments to spare so that you 'arrive' properly. Settle in your chair. Get out everything you need and then literally press the 'pause' button. Without speaking or making contact with anyone, take in a few deep breaths, assimilate what's going on around you, and sit up straight, adopting a posture which for you encapsulates the notion of noble grace.

Then tune into the room. Feel the chair beneath your thighs, a sense of yourself here in this space. Tune into your breath, noting where it starts in your body at this moment. And then tune into the energies coming out to play in the room. You don't have to spend long or labour this. The whole exercise can take just a few moments. To those around you it would appear as though you are composing yourself.

This act of 'coming into the present' is deeply empowering and centring, giving a sense of deeper presence and purpose.

Another exercise is the 3 minute Breathing Space, again worth practicing in the gap between completion and commencement of any moment of the day.

Your Beginnings & Endings
What do beginnings and endings mean for you? Think of large significant ones to date. How did you deal with them? How did you celebrate? What emotions are there in the background when you recall those times? Are you denying feeling those emotions?

Then look at your life today and see which moments stand out and why? What did you learn at the beginning and ending of those times? How have they contributed to who you are today? What qualities did they give you?

If you have a 'big' beginning and ending looming on the horizon how are you now planning on recognising this important milestone?

Bedtime Sign Off
Try tuning into your day while in bed before turning out the light, reading a book or whatever ritual you employ to prepare for the end of being awake and to call in the beginning of sleep. Watch yourself, like a film, during the day from when you awoke through to this moment. Note your interactions with those in your life that day; how you felt, thought, sensed and what you did.

Accept what you said, and what was not said, whether what you felt was 'right or wrong', or 'good or bad' and without commentary or criticism, especially of others, then let it all go, knowing that the next day is a blank sheet on which you can write again.

POST SCRIPT – STEP TEN - And now Meditate
Sit on a chair or the floor, or even lie on the floor if that is preferable, but not lying on a bed, and make contact with the ground. Make sure that your legs are uncrossed and your feet are flat on the ground. Allow your hands to settle in your lap, not clenched or clasped, possibly with one on top of the other (different spiritual schools have different thoughts about this aspect but don't get hung up about this at the start).

Then gently close your eyes, or, if this feels uncomfortable, lower the eyelids and direct your gaze gently to a spot on the floor just in front of you.

Now make contact with your face, in particular tune into your eyes; are they straining to see some imaginary screen of thoughts and images? Allow the eyes to soften. I often bring my awareness to my cheekbones to do this.

Then tune into your jawline, top and bottom; again we often clench our teeth, so soften here. It helps to drop the tongue into the well behind the bottom teeth; it is often fixed to the roof of our mouth as a constant prelude to speaking and so makes it an overused organ.

Now become aware of your posture. The spine should be straight and ideally you should be sitting away from the back of the chair so that you are self-supporting. I like the phrase 'to sit with noble grace' as my little mantra for getting into this pose. There is something beautifully ennobling about sitting in meditation.

Next bring your focus to your presence here on the floor or the chair and tune into your body as you do with the three minute breathing space, bringing awareness to where your body makes contact with the chair or ground, noting sensations, emotions, thoughts and impulses and then letting them go. Just observing without commentary, criticism or judgement.

Now it's time, as with the three minute breathing space, to make contact with your breath. Note where it comes into the body at this time and just follow it in and out, getting up close to the breath. Feel it coming in cold and going out warm. Even say to yourself, if you want: 'I am breathing in, I am breathing out'. And simply sit here with the breath.

The mind will wander, it's what minds do. You simply congratulate yourself that you have noticed you've drifted off and come back to the breath. Many meditators like to see the distracting thoughts as waves on the ocean. You are the ocean not the wave, or as clouds scudding in the sky: you are the sky not the clouds. We are not our thoughts. They come and go and like clouds or waves. We can watch them pass and return simply to following our breath... until you stop.

SECTION NOTES

STEP ONE - TREAT EACH DAY AS IF IT'S YOUR LAST

[1] Maslow's Peak Moments - Berger, 1983, p.43 (Berger, 1983)

[2] Yalom, 1980. P.91 - (Yalom, 1980)

[3] Details on the research can be found in this web article: *Be happy: Your genes may thank you for it* at http://newsroom.ucla.edu/releases/don-t-worry-be-happy-247644

STEP TWO – GO SLOWER
[1] For more details check out Earl K Miller's website earlkmiller.org

[2] Doser, R. (2015, April). *Effective-multitasking-is-an-oxymoron*. Retrieved from http://thehillnews.org:
http://thehillnews.org/features/rebeccadoser/effective-multitasking-is-an-oxymoron

[3] Hallowell M.D., E., & Ratey M.D., J. J. (2005). *Delivered From Distraction:Getting the Most out of Life with Attention Deficit Disorder*. New York: Ballantine.

[4] Information, N. C. (2015, April 2).
http://www.statisticbrain.com/attention-span-statistics/.
Retrieved from Statisticbrain.com:
http://www.statisticbrain.com/attention-span-statistics/

[5] Information, N. C. (2015, April 2).
http://www.statisticbrain.com/attention-span-statistics/.
Retrieved from Statisticbrain.com:
http://www.statisticbrain.com/attention-span-statistics/

[6] Marcus, G. (2008). *Kluge:The Haphazard Construction of the Human Mind.* New York: Houghton Mifflin Harcourt.

[7] More about Gloria Mark's fascinating work can be found on her own website here: http://www.ics.uci.edu/~gmark/Home_page/Research.html

[8] Figures around internet use are constantly being updated. A new search will reveal the latest results about traffic and email use. Basex has since been disbanded. The US research database, National Center for Biotechnology Information, is a useful port of call.

[9] Ann Pietrangelo's interesting work on nutrition and health can be found at http://www.healthline.com/health/stress/effects-on-body

[10] Key facts and statistics outlined here are covered in the article by Matthew Barbour writing in the Daily Mail on November 11, 2011: Why Eating too Quickly is a Fast Track to an Early Grave. Other resources include British Nutrition Foundation: https://www.nutrition.org.uk/nutritioninthenews/pressreleases/healthyeatingweek.html. An article in the British Medical Journal *The joint impact on being overweight of self-reported behaviours of eating quickly and eating until full: cross sectional survey* (October 2008) is also quoted in this section referring to the study at Osaka University in Japan (Department of Social and Environmental Medicine, Graduate School of Medicine, Osaka University, Japan, Oct 2008).

[11] Ibid. Daily Mail. November 11, 2011.

[12] British Nutrition Foundation: https://www.nutrition.org.uk/nutritioninthenews/pressreleases/healthyeatingweek.html. An article in the British Medical Journal *The joint impact on being overweight of self-reported behaviours of eating quickly and eating until full: cross sectional survey* (October 2008).

STEP THREE – AUTOPILOT
[1] Sadly I cannot remember where this came from. However there are a good selection of similar tales in (Reps, 2009).

STEP FOUR - HAVING A MEANINGFUL RELATIONSHIP WITH YOURSELF
[1] The definition of Mindfulness in this format by Jon Kabat-Zinn is from the Oxford Mindfulness Centre's 8 week Mindfulness Based Cognitive Therapy (MBCT) course notes but it can be found across the internet. In the bibliography you will find book titles by Kabat-Zinn particularly his seminal work *Full Catastrophe Living*.

STEP FIVE – HAVING A MEANINGFUL RELATIONSHIP WITH OTHERS
[1] Albert Mehrabian's work helped pioneer the growth of statistics and analysis in the burgeoning 1970's advertising and marketing worlds. Details are in *Silent Messages: Implicit Communication of Emotions and Attitudes* (1972).

[2] Paul D. MacLean *The Triune Brain in Evolution: role in paleocerebral functions* (1990), New York. Plenum Press.

[3] Lewis, Thomas; Amini, Fari; Lannon, Richard, *A General Theory of Love* p.63-65.

[4] Jack Kornfield. The Wise Heart: A Guide to the Universal Teachings of Buddhist Psychology (Kornfield, 2008).

STEP SIX – TOO MANY WASTED WORDS
[1] To read the full teachings of the Sufi Master Hazrat Inayat Khan the dedicated website www.wahiduddin.net is a massive resource. This quote is from Vol VII of The Gathas, 11-15.

[2] (Stephens, Atkins, & Kingston, 2009) p. 1056-1060.

[3] Again many of the modern day quotations and spiritual teachings of people like Baba Ram Dass are easily accessible online. This is from www.goodreads.com. Ram Dass' official site is https://www.ramdass.org.

STEP SEVEN – DO SOMETHING DIFFERENT EVERYDAY

[1] Although this is widely quoted by Proust from his seven-volume work, _Remembrance of Things Past_ (or _In Search of Lost Time_). The quotation above is a paraphrase of text in volume 5—_The Prisoner_—originally published in French, in 1923, and first translated into English by C. K. Moncrief.

[2] (Oliver, 2004)

STEP NINE – BEGINNINGS & ENDINGS

[1] Many thanks to Emeritus Prof. Mark Williams for giving permission to copy this extract from _Mindfulness: a practical guide to finding Peace In A Frantic World_. (Williams & Penman, 2011) p.236. It is retold from a story by Youngey Mingpur Rinpoche, _Joyful Wisdom: Embracing Change and Finding Harmony_ (Harmony, 2009).

RESOURCES

Bibliography

Barbour, M. (2011, November 11). Why Eating too Quickly is a Fast Track to an Early Grave. *Daily Mail*.

Berger, K. S. (1983). *The Developing Person Through the Life Span.* New York: Worth Publishers.

British Nutrition Foundation. (2013). *Nutrition in the News.* Retrieved from British Nutrition Foundation: https://www.nutrition.org.uk/nutritioninthenews/pressreleases/healthyeatingweek.html

Department of Social and Environmental Medicine, Graduate School of Medicine, Osaka University, Japan. (Oct 2008). The joint impact on being overweight of self reported behaviours of eating quickly and eating until full: cross sectional survey. *British Medical Journal*.

Doser, R. (2015, April). *Effective-multitasking-is-an-oxymoron*. Retrieved from http://thehillnews.org: http://thehillnews.org/features/rebeccadoser/effective-multitasking-is-an-oxymoron

earlkmiller.org. (n.d.). Retrieved from earlkmiller.org/about

Hallowell M.D., E., & Ratey M.D., J. J. (2005). *Delivered From Distraction:Getting the Most out of Life with Attention Deficit Disorder.* New York: Ballantine.

Information, N. C. (2015, April 2). *http://www.statisticbrain.com/attention-span-statistics/.* Retrieved from Statisticbrain.com: http://www.statisticbrain.com/attention-span-statistics/

Kabat-Zinn, J. (1991). *Full Catastrophe Living.* New York: Piatkus.

Kabat-Zinn, J. (1994). *Wherever You Go, There You Are.* New York: Piatkus.

RESOURCES

Kornfield, J. (2008). *The Wise Heart: A Guide to the Universal Teachings of Buddhist Psychology.* New York: Random House.

Lewis, T., Amini, F., & Lannon, R. (2000). *A General Theory of Love.* New York: Vintage.

MacLean, P. D. (1990). *The Triune Brain in Evolution: role in paleocerebral functions.* New York: Plenum Press.

Marcus, G. (2008). *Kluge:The Haphazard Construction of the Human Mind.* New York: Houghton Mifflin Harcourt.

Mark, G. (n.d.). *Home page Gloria Mark.* Retrieved from ics.uci.edu: http://www.ics.uci.edu/~gmark/Home_page/Research.html

Maslow, A. (1964). *Religions, values, and peak experiences.* London: Penguin books Limited.

Mehrabian, A. (1972). *Silent Messages: Implicit Communication of Emotions and Attitudes.* London: Wadsworth.

Oliver, M. (2004). *New & Selected Poems, Vol I.* Boston: Beacon.

Pietrangelo, A. (2014, August 25). *The Effects of Stress on the Body.* Retrieved from Healthline.com: http://www.healthline.com/health/stress/effects-on-body

Proust, M. (2006). *Rememberance of Things Past - Vol V.* London: Worsdworth.

Reps, P. (2009). *Writings From the Zen Masters.* London: Penguin.

Stephens, R., Atkins, J., & Kingston, A. (2009). Swearing As a Response to Pain. *Neuroreport*, 1056-1060.

T.S.Eliot. (2001). *Four Quartets.* London: Faber & Faber.

Wheeler, M. (2013, July 29). *Be happy: Your genes may thank you for It.* Retrieved from Newsroom UCLA: http://newsroom.ucla.edu/releases/don-t-worry-be-happy-247644

RESOURCES

Williams, M., & Penman, D. (2011). *Mindfulness: a practical guide to Finding Peace in a Frantic World.* London: piatkus.

Yalom, I.D. (1980). *Existential Psyshotherapy.* USA. Basic Books.

INDEX

INDEX

ONEFULNESS PUBLISHING

www.onefulness.com

LONDON, UK

Nine Steps to a Mindful Life (Without Meditating) –
Under the Lime Tree
Laura Payne ©2016

CPSIA information can be obtained
at www.ICGtesting.com
Printed in the USA
LVOW10s1626260717

542728LV00016B/880/P